IMAGES
of America

RESORTS OF
BERRIEN COUNTY

This is another photo of Camp Voorhees on the St. Joseph River. Note that the women and baby are well-dressed despite the primitive living conditions. (Photo courtesy of Fort Miami Heritage Society.)

Cover: The cover photo by Woodworth depicts Camp Voorhees on the St. Joseph River, *c.* 1905. Vacationers came from Chicago on steamers which landed in Benton Harbor or St. Joseph. They then boarded smaller boats, pictured in the background, which transported them to resorts or camps such as this one along the river. (Photo courtesy of Fort Miami Heritage Society.)

IMAGES
of America

RESORTS OF
BERRIEN COUNTY

Elaine Cotsirilos Thomopoulos, Ph.D.

ARCADIA

Published by Arcadia Publishing
Charleston SC, Chicago IL, Portsmouth NH, San Francisco CA

Printed in Great Britain

Library of Congress Catalog Card Number: Applied for.

For all general information contact Arcadia Publishing at:
Telephone 843-853-2070
Fax 843-853-0044
E-mail sales@arcadiapublishing.com
For customer service and orders:
Toll-Free 1-888-313-2665

Visit us on the internet at http://www.arcadiapublishing.com

This group enjoys the lazy days of summer by relaxing at Beechwood on the St. Joseph River. Note the cottages to the right and the hammock in the middle. (Photo courtesy of Fort Miami Heritage Society.)

CONTENTS

ACKNOWLEDGMENTS

The help of many people made this book go from a dream to a reality. First and foremost comes my husband, Nick, who not only encouraged me, but cheerfully accompanied me to libraries and sites to find facts and photos, and also proofread the book. I also appreciate the help of my mother, Emily Cotsirilos, my sister, Stathia Xanos, and my children, Christopher, Diana, Marie Sussman, and Melina Collins, and son-in-laws Mathieu Sussman and Joseph Collins. My cute little grandchildren, Lauren, Daniel, Jillian Sussman, and Grace Collins, renewed my energies.

Without the resources and the supportive staff of the Fort Miami Heritage Society, authoring this book would not have been possible. The Fort Miami Heritage Society allowed me to scour their archives and library and reproduce many valuable vintage photos, generously sharing these treasures with the community. Working with Matt Anderson, Kenneth Pott, Jacquie Johnson, Jennifer Gaydos, Joyce Bucholtz, and the other staff, interns, and volunteers of Fort Miami Heritage Society has been delightful. These knowledgeable, competent people enthusiastically assisted and encouraged me throughout my venture.

Once again, accolades to Jill Rauh, reference librarian at Benton Harbor Public Library, who helped me immensely by finding unusual and interesting articles in newspapers and books and allowed me use of postcards and photos from the library's collection. She and the other friendly library staff made me feel at home. The same can be said of Mary Kynast and the staff at St. Joseph/Maud Preston Palenske Memorial Library and Jane Ward of the Three Oaks Township Library. The library staff gave me technical assistance and permission to reproduce images. The courteous staff of the New Buffalo and Bridgman Libraries also assisted me. Librarians are wonderful!

Institutions and businesses in both Michigan and Illinois also helped by giving me technical assistance, allowing access to resources, or lending photos. They include the American Sokol Organization, Archives and Regional History Collections of Western Michigan University, Berrien County Historical Association, Bridgman Chamber of Commerce, Chicago Historical Society Research Center, Chicago Archives of the Spertus Museum, Chicago Commons, Deer Forest, Evanston Historical Society, Fort St. Joseph Museum, Gintaras Resort, Gordon Beach Inn, Grand Beach, Harbor Country Chamber of Commerce, The Inn at Union Pier, Jesse Owens Foundation, Jewish Historical Society of Michigan, Krasl Art Center, Kilwins, Lakeside Inn, Mary's City of David, Michigan Maritime Museum, Milda's Corner Market, New Buffalo Yacht Club, North Berrien Historical Society Museum, Pennellwood Resort, Prairie Club, River's Edge Bed and Breakfast, St. Chrysostom Episcopalian Church, St. Joseph Today, Sarett Nature Center, Snowflake Motel, Soni Springs Camp, Southwestern Michigan Tourist Council, Sweethaven, Three Oaks Spokes Bicycle Museum, Tower Hill Camp, and Wilkinson Museum.

The people of Berrien County are passionate about their history. Many people from Berrien County, as well as those from the Chicago area, told me their fascinating stories about resorts or second homes, allowed me to reproduce photographs or postcards (which are acknowledged at the end of each caption), scanned photos, shared their knowledge of the community, or helped me by proofreading the manuscript. Bob Rosenbaum was one of the first people to guide me. I used scores of images from his extensive collection of Southwest Michigan postcards. He also shared his library and wisdom with me.

The other marvelous people who assisted me and to whom I am very grateful include Mary Almer, Ray Almer, Ted Bachunas, Helen Bachunas, Bob Beaver, Merry J.B. Bolt, Devereux Bowly, Rose Cervenka, Liora Cobin, Joyce Collier, Barbara Cohen, Kosta Dalageorgas, Jacquie Dziak, Sophe Fatouras, Kym Fischer, Jerry Foust, Linda Goddard, Betty Goetz, Leo Goodsell, Robert Gouwens, Dick Grau, Elizabeth Hahn, Herb Hahn, Marty Helsman, Chris Hilton, Judy Jackson, Bill Jann, Joyce Jann, Floyd Jergon, Ruth Jergon, Joe Johnson, Nicole Jacoby, Linas Johansonas, Milda Rudaitis Johansonas, Pete Jorgensen, Gintaras Karaitis, Ann Keech, Judy Kreston Lahm, John Lamping, Chriss Lyon, Bernard McGill, Tom McFarland, Ruth Magdzinski, Jane Granzow Miles, Bob Myers, Chuck Nelson, Pradyuman Patel, Janie Peterson, Natalie Plee, Nick Poulos, Marlene Owens Rankin, Rick Rasmussen, John Rassogianis, Rich Ray, Maggie Richter, Bernie Rizzo, Mary Robertson, Marjorie Royce, Annette Schabowski, Rob Schmidt, Daryl Schlender, Dan Schneider, Sara Shambarger, Jack Sizer, Margie Souliotis, David Stacey, Ron Taylor, Judy Whittier, Connie F. Williams, John Wilson Jr., John Wilson Sr., Christine Wright, Susan VanBragt, Anne Vandermolen, Andy Vavra, Richard Vavra, Bryan Volstrof, and Seymour Zaban. Thanks also to Maura Brown, my editor at Arcadia Publishing, who did a great job in making sure the book was in tip-top shape for publication. I tried to keep track of all the wonderful people who helped me but I apologize if I failed to include someone.

ST. JOSEPH - BENTON HARBOR

The caption on this postcard reads, "Beautiful apple blossoms spread their delicate fragrance across the countryside in early May. Western Michigan has long been known as the garden spot of the Midwest. Tempered by Lake Michigan this area has an ideal climate to bring out the best in flavor and quality." Since the 1860s, the luscious fruit of Southwestern Michigan has attracted visitors, as noted in this letter sent on August 3, 1868, to the *Chicago Republican:* "I want to call the attention of your city readers . . . to the advantages of this locality. Some fine day step on board the steamer *Comet*, Capt. Napier, at Goodrich's wharf, at 10 o'clock, and after a delightful trip of five hours, you will find yourselves at the town of St. Joseph, a place well known as the center of the great fruit-growing regions of Michigan, and the place of shipment for its hundreds of thousands of baskets of peaches and tons of berries. The afternoon may be spent in looking about town, spending the night at the hotel, and in the morning take a team at the livery stable for a day's ride." (Postcard courtesy of Fort Miami Heritage Society.)

INTRODUCTION

At the turn of the century, thousands of visitors traveled to Berrien County in Southwest Michigan to escape the sweltering summer heat and crowded cities—delighting in the cool breezes off Lake Michigan. Through more than 200 photos dating from the 1880s to the present, this enchanting volume tells the stories of the lazy summers on the beaches and in the countryside of Southwest Michigan. It chronicles the jaunts, not only of the upper-class industrialists and their families who first traveled to Michigan at the turn of the century and bought second homes there, but also of the working-class and the ethnic groups who discovered the area in the 1920s and 1930s.

The ethnic resort communities (including those of Irish, Czechoslovakian, Swedish, Jewish, African, Greek, Italian, Polish, and Lithuanian descent) were scattered in various enclaves throughout the area—from the Irish second-home community of Grand Beach (near Indiana) to the Jewish resorts in Benton Harbor.

Whatever their ethnicity, the summer visitors spent lazy summer days swimming in Lake Michigan, rowing boats down the calm St. Joseph River, picking vegetables and delicious peaches, berries, cherries, apples, pears, and grapes in the farms to the east, and watching the sun set while they sang around the campfire. They relished three hearty meals a day at luxurious lakeside resorts, such as the 175-bed Golfmore Hotel at Grand Beach, or roughed it at campsites or primitive cabins at farms in Sodus or Berrien Springs, cooking over a fire or kerosene stove. They came for their health, drinking the cool mineral waters of Eastman Springs in Benton Harbor or soaking in the pungent sulphur baths in St. Joseph or Benton Harbor hotels. The proprietors boasted that the baths could cure, "rheumatism, nervous disorders, and poor circulation." Families brought the children for a healthier outdoor way of life, away from the dirt, disease, and dangers of the city.

Even without television, children did not complain of being bored. They could swim, boat, fish, explore the woods, or play childhood games. Most came with their families, but some attended camps, including the Chicago Commons Camp, Jewish and Czechoslovakian camps, scout and YWCA camps, or church camps such as Tower Hill, Warren, or First Church Camps.

Excitement radiates in the early photos of the luxurious steamer ships bringing vacationers across Lake Michigan to St. Joseph and Benton Harbor. Those going to the country resorts would be picked up by horse and wagon or would travel down the St. Joseph River via riverboats such as the *May Graham*. Trains also transported travelers from Chicago and Indiana, with train stations found in each of the small resort towns. By the early 20th century, the local interurban electric trains transported people from St. Joseph and Benton Harbor to vacation destinations as far as Berrien Springs or Paw Paw Lake. Early photos show wives and children waiting at the train stations for husbands to join them on weekends. Beginning in the 1920s and 1930s, with improved roads, cars became a preferred method of transportation, and by the 1950s, motels were built to accommodate the highway drivers.

Whichever way they traveled, it was an experience full of laughter, fun, and anticipation—anticipation not only for the lovely beaches and countryside, but also for the amusement parks of Silver Beach in St. Joseph, the House of David in Benton Harbor, or Deer Forest in Coloma, whose friendly deer still delight children today. Silver Beach had a boardwalk, a beautiful, sandy beach, a roller coaster, and a dance pavilion. Silver Beach closed in the early 1970s. Today the beach is a county park and rated one of the ten best beaches in the nation by *Parents* magazine.

The House of David, a Benton Harbor religious community, built an amusement park in 1908 and operated it until 1973. Its myriad attractions included a zoo, miniature trains which traveled a mile around the park, hot-rod cars for children, musical performances, and baseball games played by the bearded House of David team. One vacationer recalls the thrill of seeing Satchel Paige (the first African-American player to be admitted to the Baseball Hall of Fame) play.

In the 1930s and 1940s, loving couples danced to the big bands at pavilions such as Shadowland and Crystal Palace. The big bands included Louis "Satchmo" Armstrong, Wayne King, Jimmy Dorsey, Tommy Dorsey, Les Brown, Duke Ellington, Woody Herman, and Count Basie.

Famous men of the past, like Al Capone, Jesse Owens, Carl Sandburg, Joe Louis, Mayor Anton Cermak, and Mayor Richard J. Daley have enjoyed the attractions of Berrien County. Present-day notables who have second homes in the area include Mayor Richard M. Daley, Reverend Andrew Greeley, and many TV personalities including Andy Shaw, Walter Jacobson, Roger Ebert, and Robert Jordan. For more than 100 years, city folk have come to Southwest Michigan to savor all the pleasures it offers: the beautiful trees, colorful wildflowers and chirping birds, the ever-changing colors of the sunset bathing the lake with a pinkish glow, the lulling sound of waves at bedtime, the smell of strawberries, the breath of fresh air, and the friendly down-to-earth people.

The *City of Milwaukee*, bringing tourists, pulls into the E.A. Graham Docks in 1896. *Andy*, the tugboat, is beside her. The *City of Milwaukee* was called the "Honeymoon Ship." (Photo courtesy of Fort Miami Heritage Society.)

This is U.S. 12 looking north near New Buffalo, probably in the 1930s. Car travel to Michigan soon replaced travel by train and boat. In 1928, M-11 was designated U.S. Highway 12. After World War II, they renamed it the Red Arrow Highway to honor the Army's 32nd division (the Red Arrow Division). Many young Michigan men fought bravely with that division in both World Wars I and II. The division became known as "Red Arrow" because of their swift assaults through German lines in World War I. In World War II, the division received a commendation from General Douglas MacArthur. The State Line Rest Lodge opened in 1935 at 19135 U.S.12, in south New Buffalo Township, becoming the first such lodge in the state. During its first seven months, more than 30,000 visitors, representing 48 states and 12 foreign countries, were registered as guests. Driving to Michigan was half the fun for some. James Tatooles, who was interviewed in a project conducted by the Berrien Country Historical Association and Columbia College Chicago, describes the three-hour trip (before the existence of the I-294 and I-94), "You would think we were like vagabonds. I mean everybody would be loaded in the car. I would be sitting on my grandmother's lap because there wasn't enough room in the car for everybody to have a seat." Another interviewee, Celia Alexopoulos, recalls the trip, "We'd sing school songs and old folk songs and the Greek and American national anthems. And reminisce about the early times, with parents telling their stories about growing up in Greece. It was a happy occasion riding in the car." (Postcard courtesy of Robert Rosenbaum.)

One

RESORTS NEAR LAKE MICHIGAN

SAND DUNE ON THE SHORE OF LAKE MICHIGAN, BENTON HARBOR, MICH.

Lake Michigan came into existence about 2,000 years ago at the end of the last major glaciation. It is the third largest of the Great Lakes and sixth largest lake in the world. Southwest Michigan beaches feature sand dunes such as these, something seen in few other places in the U.S. From a Warren Dunes State Park brochure comes this explanation of the formation of the sand dunes, "Magnificent sand dunes—the trademark of our state park—were formed over years of geological time. Receding glaciers, thousands of feet thick, scraped the continental bedrock of Michigan. The tremendous weight of the ice scoured the material, reducing it down to what we see today. A combination of wind and water deposited the sand grains, composed of 90% quartz, along the western shore of Michigan, forming the majestic dunes of today." The unique characteristic of the dunes of Southwest Michigan is a squeaking noise produced as one walks along the wet sand, prompting some to call them "singing sands." Note the boat on Lake Michigan's horizon, a favorite means of transportation for visitors from Chicago during the early 20th century. (Postcard courtesy of Fort Miami Heritage Society.)

This Bill Jasch home originally served as a sales center for the Long Beach Development Company. It later became the residence of sales agent LeRoy Cole and his family. The Long Beach Development Company developed a resort community that stretches across the Indiana and Michigan border. It is called Michiana Shores on the Indiana side and Michiana on the Michigan side. The company began subdividing and building on 600 acres in the 1920s, developing slightly later than surrounding communities because of the swampy and heavily wooded land. Resorters paid as little as $1,000 for a lot with a summer cottage in the 1920s and 1930s. Bill Jasch built more than 60 homes in Michiana in the 1930s and 1940s. He constructed the homes of smooth, finished logs, usually painted brown, with low eaves that reminded him of the chalets of his native Switzerland. Michiana attracted Jewish residents—unlike other communities on the coast of Lake Michigan, the Long Beach Development Company did not prohibit the sale of land to Jews. Until the Supreme Court ruled against it in 1948, many communities used restrictive covenants that prohibited the sale of land or homes to African Americans and Jews. (Photo by Elaine Thomopoulos.)

This 1928 arch proclaims "New Buffalo: The Gateway of Michigan." The arch spanned the intersection of Buffalo and Willard Street in New Buffalo. The dedication took place on April 26, 1928, with many state and local officials attending. The Businessmen's Association sponsored the dedication and also led the effort to erect the arch. The Harbor Country Chamber of Commerce has replaced the Businessmen's Association. Harbor Country is a trademarked geographic region which encompasses not only New Buffalo, but Michiana, Grand Beach, Union Pier, Lakeside, Harbert, Sawyer, and, slightly inland, Three Oaks. Beginning at the Michigan state line, these tightly knit communities encompass a stretch of about 15 miles north along Lake Michigan and six miles inland. (Postcard courtesy of Robert Rosenbaum.)

Judy's Log Cabin Motel on U.S. 12 became a popular vacation spot during the 1950s. Cabins and motels like this one lined Route 12 (Red Arrow Highway) and attracted thousands of visitors from Chicago and Gary. Judy's Motel and the adjacent Hilltop Motel had knotty pine interiors and the accommodations included: kitchenettes, air-conditioning, heating, and an outdoor pool. The pool boasted an underwater observation window. The motels were owned and managed by Mr. and Mrs. Norman Lubke and their children, Judy and David. (Postcard courtesy of Robert Rosenbaum)

Even during prohibition, vacationers had a steady supply of alcohol. This 1928 photo shows the sheriff and his deputies at the site of a moonshine still in Berrien County, probably in New Buffalo. Pictured here are "Curley" Phairas (trustee), Sheriff Fred Bryant, Deputy Frank Priebe, Deputy Erwin Kubath, Chet Overcash, and Charles Johnson (deputy in New Buffalo). (Photo courtesy of Fort Miami Heritage Society.)

This is where the Galien River in New Buffalo empties into Lake Michigan, quite a change from what it looks like now. (Postcard courtesy of Robert Rosenbaum.)

This is the Red Cedar Tap Room of Calvin's Grill in New Buffalo, a popular hangout for summer visitors and local people. John Calvin opened the Calvin Grill and sold it to the Pappas family years later. (Postcard courtesy of Robert Rosenbaum.)

In this 1997 photo are, from left to right: Sophe Fatouras, owner of 105 East Grill in New Buffalo; Robert Jordan, CBS newscaster with a second home in Union Pier; and Barbara Smith, from Indiana. Jordan is one of many media personalities who have purchased second homes in Berrien County. Others include Roger Ebert, Walter Jacobson, Joan Esposito, Andy Shaw, Ron Magers, Father Andrew Greeley, Steve Dahl, Paul Hogan, Rick Kogan, Carol Marin, Robin Robinson, and Gene Siskel. (Photo courtesy of Sophe Fatouras.)

The New Buffalo Yacht Club, one of the organizations instrumental in getting a harbor for New Buffalo, was organized in 1956 when a group of 25 people met at the Rio Restaurant to discuss how to help maintain and develop New Buffalo's harbor. According to the *New Buffalo Story*, the marina got started when Harold and William Guhl offered two boats for rent and live bait for sale in 1947. This grew into today's dredged harbor with moorings on both sides of the bridge as well as condominium developments that include housing on land as well as boat moorings. The Chamber of Commerce first started raising money for the harbor in 1954, with the Lions contributing in 1954, and the New Buffalo Yacht Club holding a benefit in 1957. Although the drawings of the proposed refuge Harbor were unveiled in 1961, because of various delays, construction wasn't started until 1973. The New Buffalo Harbor was dedicated during 1976, bringing new vitality to the area. (Photo courtesy of the New Buffalo Yacht Club.)

There were three different locations for the railroad depot in Grand Beach: south of the Vetterly farm, in front of their home, and the gate area south of the fourth green. Husbands who worked in the city would take the train from the city to join their families on weekends. (Photo courtesy of Village of Grand Beach.)

Richard L. Whitton on the
First Tee
GRAND BEACH MICH.

According to a booklet published by the Harbor Country Chamber of Commerce, Grand Beach's golf course dates to 1911. Famous golf course designer, Tom Bendelow, laid out the initial nine-hole course. A clubhouse, built the same year, offered overnight accommodations. The next year, a bowling alley was added. Golfers came from Chicago via the Michigan Central Railroad, which stopped outside of Grand Beach two or three times a day. In 1942, the golf course was offered to the village. (Photo courtesy of Village of Grand Beach.)

This image was taken on the shore in Grand Beach; the Golfmore Hotel is in the background. Floyd Perkins originally purchased approximately 600 acres bordering Lake Michigan near the Indiana border, known as Grand Beach, in the early 1900s. He planned to establish it as a site for a shooting preserve. Eventually he and his partner, George Ely, decided to form the Grand Beach Company and promote the area as a resort community instead. Perkins and Ely bought parcel after parcel of tax-title land until they had four miles of beach. To build the resort, thousands of trees were cut down. The Village of Grand Beach was incorporated in 1934. In the 1940s and 1950s, Grand Beach became a family-oriented summer gathering place for the Irish, who came mostly from the south side of Chicago. They enjoyed each other's company on the beach, on the golf course, at lively, fun-filled parties at the community center, or in their cottages. They also attended outdoor Catholic masses on the golf course. Some of Grand Beach's famous Irish American residents include Mayors Richard J. and Richard M. Daley of Chicago and author and sociologist Rev. Andrew Greeley. Grand Beach remains a resort community and is still enjoyed by some of the same families who bought cottages there in the 1940s and 1950s. (Photo courtesy of Fort Miami Heritage Society.)

Here is a listing of early residents of Grand Beach. Nearly all of the 33 members are from the city of Chicago, with three from the suburbs and one from Jacksonville. In 1915 all homeowners were instructed to name their cottages. This was repeated again in 1935. (Image courtesy of Village of Grand Beach.)

"A Grand Beach Home", Grand Beach, Mich.   10-gbmr

The early homes of the well-to-do included three homes built c. 1916 by Frank Lloyd Wright: the Ernest Vosburgh House, the W.S. Carr House, and the Joseph J. Bagley House. To accommodate the middle class, Grand Beach Company brought 20 Sears and Roebuck catalogue cottages to the area, some of which can still be seen. Residents also bought cottages that were originally built for those who had been employed at the Golfmore Hotel, which burned down in 1939. (Postcard courtesy of the Village of Grand Beach.)

This is the brochure for the annual ski tournament conducted on January 10, 1926 at Grand Beach. Near the hotel, on one of the dunes, was a ski lift. Every year, for several years, beginning in 1922, the Grand Beach Ski Club held a ski tournament which attracted skiers from throughout the nation. This is the cover of the program book for the Fourth Annual Tournament in 1926. About 60 expert skiers competed, with judges awarding prizes. (Image courtesy of the Village of Grand Beach.)

FOURTH ANNUAL

SKI TOURNAMENT

January 10th, 1926

GRAND BEACH SKI CLUB

GRAND BEACH, MICHIGAN

Ski Slide, Hotel Golfmore, Grand Beach, Mich.

This postcard shows the ski slide to the left, adjacent to Hotel Golfmore in Grand Beach. (Postcard courtesy of Robert Rosenbaum.)

The 175-room Golfmore Hotel was located in a beautiful lakeside setting in Grand Beach near the Indiana border. The resort, which opened in 1922, served three meals a day. Activities included a 27-hole golf course, dancing, concerts, tennis, and horseback riding. Guests used various types of boats: sailboats, powerboats, canoes, skiffs, and water bicycles. They swam or played water polo. For winter recreation, a ski jump was built on one of the dunes. Unfortunately, the hotel burned down in 1939. (Image courtesy of Village of Grand Beach.)

These guests enjoy a leisurely game of croquet at the elegant Golfmore Hotel. (Photo courtesy of Village of Grand Beach.)

According to an article in *The Red Arrow Review*, Joe and Julia Fischer ran this hotel in the early 1900s. This building was one of the three buildings that became the Karonsky's Hotel and that is now the Inn at Union Pier. Louis and Sarah Karonsky added two buildings to the original hotel. Karonsky's Hotel, also known by the Yiddish name *Scheine Vista* (Beautiful View), was the only kosher hotel in Union Pier. Still evident on the front doorpost is the *mezuzah*, a small container which holds Deuteronomy 6:4-9 and Deuteronomy 11:13-21 written on parchment. To accommodate Jewish resort guests in Union Pier during the summer, there were two synagogues on Lakeshore Road. Karonsky's offered 39 tiny rooms with iron beds and dressers (some refurbished and still in use at The Inn), as well as six bathrooms and an outdoor shower. The hotel operated until the 1970s. Bill and Madeleine Reinke purchased it in 1983, and after renovating all three buildings, the Inn became one of the first bed and breakfasts in the area. Bill and Joyce Jann now own it. In contrast to Karonsky's establishment, the Inn now has 16 spacious guest rooms, all with private baths, and most of the rooms have wood-burning Swedish fireplaces called *kakelugns*. The Janns have broadened the scope of the bed and breakfast by offering dinner-cabaret weekends during the winters. As captivating as the entertainment, is the Inn's ghost story. While Joyce and Bill Jann caution that the facts in the story have not yet been confirmed by research, according to what they have been told, in the 1920s or 1930s, a Chicago couple and their young son rented a room at the hotel. Supposedly, the boy drowned when he was washed off a pier by a large wave. Joyce reports that on a few occasions guests have commented about hearing a child bouncing a ball in the hallway, even though there weren't any children at the inn. (Photo courtesy of Bill and Joyce Jann of the Inn at Union Pier.)

This is the Karonsky's Dining Room before it was refurbished and transformed into the Great Room at the Inn at Union Pier. Note the piano to the left. The Great Room now has a Steinway grand piano and comfortable couches and chairs. In the Great Room, guests relax with a good book, converse with friends, or play games such as chess or checkers. A private dining room, added in the 1980s, seats guests for a delicious full breakfast. The Janns treat guests to wine and popcorn in the evenings. (Photo courtesy of Bill and Joyce Jann of the Inn at Union Pier.)

Lake View Hotel from M 11, Union Pier, Mich.   40703 nr

The Lake View Hotel in Union Pier has long been the gathering place for various groups, including members of Jewish and Polish communities. In the 1970s, the hotel was purchased by a group of friends who share the pleasure of living across the street from Lake Michigan. (Postcard courtesy of Robert Rosenbaum.)

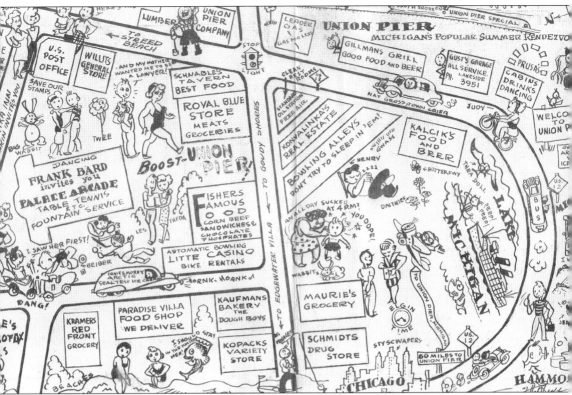

This map of Union Pier illustrates many of the businesses operating there in the 1940s. The area had developed into a resort community, with thousands of tourists and second home people swelling the population in the summers. The first summer resorter came in the 1880s. She was Mrs. Nancy Avery, according to Mrs. H.W. Gowdy in her article in the *Union Pier Wave*. By the late 1890s Cecil Richards built a house which was later occupied by the M.J. Collins family. Gowdy reports, "By 1901 Gowdy's Beach was platted by Franklin and Herbert Gowdy. In 1906 there were eight families resorting here—the Richards, Andersons, Synders, Camps, Newtons, Van Burens, Hopkins, and McCords. The O'Brien, Varga and Bilek houses were the only ones for rent to summers people." In another *Union Pier Wave* article, "Bohemia Settlement," written in 1933, Gowdy noted that the eastern portion of the district had been settled by Czechoslovakians from Chicago, who built many hotel and boarding houses. She says the following families opened their homes to paying guests: The Koutnicks, Vavras, Shotkas, Kuceras, Krkarecs, Schnabls, Gallas, Bileks, and Krestans. Ruth Magdzinski remembers resorts owned by the Prusa, Kreston, Soucek, Mareska, and Vavra families. The Jewish community also had a presence in Union Pier from the beginning of the century into the 1950s. By the 1960s, African Americans and Lithuanians had discovered the pleasures of the sunny shores of Union Pier's Lake Michigan. Now Union Pier has become a community that appeals to young professionals from Chicagoland, with many of the little summer cottages now converted to year-round second homes. Scores of construction workers are on the scene, either rehabbing or building new homes. (Image courtesy of Robert Rosenbaum.)

For many decades, Czech families enjoyed the Vavra Resort in Union Pier. Pictured are members of the Wolf, Barta, and Czech families, with Pally the dog, The Vavra Resort had seven housekeeping cottages. Five of them had outhouses and water that required pumping. The outhouses were in use until the early 1980s when the resort closed. According to Andy Vavra, the grandson of the owners, even though some of the resort families were well-to-do and could afford better accommodations, they enjoyed living the simple life in the country, hanging out at the beach all day. The families would come year after year, up to 40 or 50 years in a row. Even though the children left their comfortable homes in the city to rough it in the country, the summers the children spent at the resort were the best times of their lives. The Vavra Resort has now been transformed into the delightful Sweethaven Resort. (Photo courtesy of the Sweethaven Resort.).

This outhouse at the Vavra Resort served the two connected cottages called the Twins. Guests used the outhouses until the early 1980s when the resort closed. The former Vavra Resort is now operated as the Sweethaven Resort, with modern bathrooms and attractive accommodations. (Photo courtesy of the Sweethaven Resort.)

The Store, 1957

The Vavra Store used to be the Union Pier schoolhouse. It was moved to the Vavra property by horses in 1928, after the new school was built. The new school only lasted a couple of years, since Union Pier and New Buffalo were consolidated into one district. The new school was leased to eight community clubs at $1 per year. (Photo courtesy of the Sweethaven Resort.)

The postcard reads: "Prusa's Café and Tourist Cabins, Open all Year U.S. 12, Union Pier." The Prusa family owned a large dance hall and cabins on Red Arrow, which is now Miller's Country House, as well as a gas station, which is now the Wine Seller. These buildings also housed J's Café, the Flim Flam Club, and the Wayside Inn. During the war years and just afterward, it became very popular; people lined up outside, anxious to dance to the big bands. Ruth Magdzinski recalls dancing at the local dance halls, including the White Palace, which had one of the best dance floors in the area. In the 1940s, jitterbug dance contests would be held, and Magdzinski says that the country kids always marveled at the expertise of the Chicago kids. (Postcard courtesy of Robert Rosenbaum.)

The Gordon Beach Inn, although completely remodeled, continues to retain the feeling of the 1920s resort pictured here. Dr. Louis Gordon built the Gordon Beach Inn after he faced discrimination as a Jew. Devereux Bowly, the current owner of the inn, tells the story on the Lakeside Inn website (Lakesideinns.com): "Dr. Louis Gordon, a physician from Chicago, had been in the habit of renting a house each summer at Rush's Cottages, a Jewish enclave a little north of the hotel. In the early 1920s, anti-Jewish sentiment became so rabid that fences were employed on each side of Rush's beach, to confine their guests. Signs were put up reading 'No Dogs or Jews Allowed.' Merchants were pressured not to deliver food or other provisions to Jewish families in Lakeside. . . . Things became so bad that Dr. Gordon and several other Jewish businessmen contracted to purchase an apple orchard in Union Pier, a mile and one-half south of Lakeside, with plans to develop it as the Gordon Beach subdivision. The rest of the investors ultimately dropped out of the venture, but Dr. Gordon carried out the project himself, including constructing the Gordon Beach Inn in two stages in 1925 and 1929. Union Pier developed a large Jewish-American population, and after World War II, a significant African-American and Lithuanian-American presence." Unfortunately, in 1967 three white youth used Molotov cocktails on two African-American-owned resorts, one of them being Miller's Gordon Beach Inn. The other resort, Gun's Tourist Home and Motel, suffered little damage, but the fire at the Gordon Beach Inn completely destroyed its second story. An article in *The New Buffalo Times* quotes a resident as saying, "I have always felt welcome here and have been well-treated by everyone. Of course you can't always tell how people really feel. We have had minor troubles in the past three summers with name calling, throwing of bricks and the painting of swastikas on our property, but its always outsiders who cause it." The paper goes on to state, "For the past several years a number of Negro families have quietly moved into the Gowdy Shores and the Gordon Beach areas of Union Pier. They bought run-down resorts and homes and it is generally accepted that the properties were improved and beautified by the new owners." (Postcard courtesy of Robert Rosenbaum.)

The Libuse Inn on Townline Road was operated by Charles and Tillie Mrizek, who moved to Union Pier from Cicero, Illinois, in 1926. Mrizek changed his surname to Barr because he felt would be better for business and the resort became known as the Barr Resort. Jim Barr remembers that Czech people used to come by Greyhound bus from Chicago to spend weekends there in the 1930s. Ruth Madgzinski recalls, "Buses filled with tourists would come for a day in the country, going to the beach, relaxing, and then settling down to a good meal of duck, sauerkraut, and dumplings with Kolache for dessert." In the late 1930s the resort began catering to Jews. Jim would drive the resorters back and forth to Barr's Beach, which was nearby, on the other side of the Red Arrow Highway. His parents partnered with Charlie Konvalinka to build 11 cottages, named Lake Villa Cottages, right on the lake *c.* 1934. (Postcard courtesy of Robert Rosenbaum.)

This postcard states: "Waiting for Week-end Friends at the Station, Union Pier." Often mothers and their children would stay in Michigan for weeks or months at a time, to be joined by their husbands, who arrived via train on Friday nights. This occurred in most of the small resort towns, since at that time trains like the Pere Marquette made frequent stops. Chicagoans also took the South Shore train to Michigan City, which started limited service in 1912. The South Shore bus took passengers from the station to the towns along the lake, all the way to Benton Harbor. Today the South Shore bus no longer exists, although the South Shore train continues its run from Chicago to Michigan City. Amtrak trains stop at St. Joseph, New Buffalo, and Niles. As roads became better and automobiles more reliable and affordable, driving became the preferred method of transportation. (Postcard courtesy of Robert Rosenbaum.)

Olympic star Jesse Owens (pictured at far right) celebrates his birthday at his second home in Union Pier. Also pictured (from left) are the son of Owens' Olympic teammate Dave Albritton, and a grand-nephew of Jesse Owens, Arish Roundtree III. Owens lived in Chicago when he and his wife Ruth bought their second home in Union Pier in 1969. Owens' three daughters, Gloria O. Hemphill, Beverly O. Prather and Marlene O. Rankin and their families take delight in the home and continue to organize family reunions every few years, with children and grandchildren joining them from Arizona, New York, and Washington. Marlene O. Rankin writes, "The property was intended to be a retreat for the entire Owens family. [My parents] particularly wanted their five grandchildren to have a place where they could spend quality time together. The property has been a source of pleasure and pride to all of us. There have been two weddings, graduation parties, engagement announcements, birthday parties, Thanksgiving dinners, New Year's Celebrations, and of course, celebration of all the major summer holidays. Though we have suffered a number of significant family losses—Jesse Owens in 1980, Ruth Owens in 2001 and more recently Donald Prather (son-in-law) in 2004—the country is a place where they are close to us and the memories warm and comforting." Until the 1960s, just a few African Americans lived in Union Pier. When Jewish residents started selling their cottages, African Americans from Chicago and Gary, as well as Lithuanians, bought them. African Americans had been coming to Berrien Country for vacations since early in the century, as noted in an article published in the *News-Palladium* on August 10, 1909. The headline reads, "Colored Folk Have a Resort." Stockholders from Benton Harbor, Indianapolis, St. Louis, and Evanston, Illinois organized under the name West Michigan Resort Company. The article states, "The company filed articles of incorporation at the county clerk's office and was organized to induce wealthy and respectable colored persons to invest in Michigan real estate and to make their summer homes here. The company has purchased the old Sampson farm, northeast of the city [Benton Harbor] near Pottawatomie Park and about fifty guests are at present stopping there." (Photo courtesy of the Jesse Owens Foundation.)

Juozas Rudzinskas (left), Algirdas Karaitis (center), and Jurgis Janusaitis (right), writer for the Lithuanian newspaper *Draugas*, enjoy each other's company at the Gintaras Resort on Lakeshore Road in Union Pier. The Gintaras Resort opened its doors to Lithuanian guests in 1960 after Algirdas and Viktoria Karaitis purchased the estate of Paul Gray Hoffman, the former chairman of the board at the Studebaker-Packard Corporation. The Karaitises, who came to the United States as "displaced persons" in 1949, yearned for a respite from working seven days a week, 8:00 a.m. to 10:00 p.m., at their the Brighton Park grocery store. The beautiful five-acre estate on Lake Michigan afforded them that opportunity. The property reminded them of the shore of the Baltic Sea in Lithuania. It included a luxurious nine-bedroom home overlooking the lake, servants' quarters, a log home, and a tennis court. The Karaitises transformed the buildings to accommodate resort guests, and their son, Gintaras, and daughter, Ausrine, assisted in running the resort. Guests enjoyed tasty Lithuanian meals, swimming, sunbathing, games, Friday night bonfires on the tennis court, and talent shows complete with Lithuanian songs and accordion music. Gintaras Karaitis, who moved to the resort when he was 10 years old, took over the operation of the resort after his father's death in 1996. He now runs it with his wife, Chris. He remembers: "You could barely walk down the streets of Union Pier because there were so many Lithuanians." He estimates that about 98 percent of their clientele were Lithuanian. Today he says it is about 10 percent. Other Lithuanian-owned resorts of the past included Lengvinas, Rambynas (Gordon Beach Inn), Ruta, Dimgaila, Egle (Evergreen), Neringa (now Firefly), and Venta. The Lithuanian presence is still very evident in Union Pier. Visitors to the two Lithuanian businesses on Townline Road, Milda's Corner Market and G and K Party Store (which replaced earlier Lithuanian-owned stores named Neringa and Vilija), will see dozens of Lithuanian customers, many of whom now live in the Union Pier area full-time. (Photo courtesy of the Gintaras Resort.)

This photo, taken in August 1972, shows avid chess players awaiting the moves of Tautvaisa, a Chess Master from Chicago. He came to the Gintaras Resort for the summers and used to hold tournaments where he would play more than 20 people. "He went around playing with a drink in his hand, and usually beat all his competitors," said Gintaras Karaitis. Believing in being physically fit as well as mentally alert, Tautvaisa swam out on the lake half the day and then swam back the rest of the day. Another group, the Lithuanian Architects and Engineers, met annually at the resort in the 1960s. They presented lectures in the Lithuanian language. (Photo courtesy of the Gintaras Resort.)

At the Gintaras Resort, a Jesuit priest from the Chicago area celebrated the Catholic Lithuanian Mass each Sunday on the grass facing the lake. This took place during the 1970s and 1980s. (Photo courtesy of the Gintaras Resort.)

The Gintaras Resort at 15860 Lakeshore Road in Union Pier was previously the estate of Paul Gray Hoffman, who was the administrator of the Economic Cooperation Administration (the Marshall Plan), president and director of the Ford Foundation, and chairman of the board of the Studebaker-Packard corporation. Hoffman's guests are said to have included Madam Chiang Kai-shek, Bob Hope, Bing Crosby, and Gypsy Rose Lee. Other notables who had homes north of Hoffman's estate, in Lakeside, include Harold Swift of Swift Packing Company and president of the board at the University of Chicago, and the Rueckheims. The Rueckheim brothers, F.W. and Louis, introduced a sweet snack that became known as Cracker Jack at the Columbian Exposition of 1893. Traveling down Lakeshore Road in Lakeside, visitors can identify streets named Swift Lane and Cracker Jack Lane. (Photo courtesy of the Gintaras Resort.)

31

This is a vintage postcard of the Lakeside Park Inn in Lakeside. The Aylesworth family developed this property into a resort. After Mr. Aylesworth died of smallpox, his son Arthur was summoned home to help his mother care for the resort. Within a few years, Arthur became the owner. A colorful character and world traveler, Arthur produced films about game hunting in South America, toured with Buffalo Bill's Wild West Show, and operated a gambling hall and bar in Las Vegas. According to the resort's current owner, Devereux Bowly, the Lakeside Inn became very popular in the 1920s. African-American waiters who worked at the Palmer House in Chicago came to work at the resort in the summer. Guests spent their days hanging out at the beach or visiting the miniature zoo, which included a pet bear, deer, goats, and peacocks. Dancing, gambling, and liquor—even during Prohibition—made the evenings exciting. Supposedly, bootleggers' boats from Canada would beach themselves in front of the inn and guests would wade out into the lake to help unload the cases of whiskey. Despite financial difficulties, Arthur Aylesworth held on to the property until the 1950s, when he lost it because of foreclosure. A few years later, Bob Creevy bought the resort and installed a baby clothing factory in the ballroom, still renting rooms upstairs during the summer. The internationally-known print dealer, John Wilson, and his wife, Kay, purchased the inn in 1968. Wilson ran his print business out of several rooms on the main floor of the inn and converted the building in the rear into studio space. Artists from around the world stayed there during the summer, and it became known as Lakeside Center for the Arts. During the art center's early years, visiting Chicago-based artists included Richard Hunt, Ed Paschke, and Roger Brown, all of whom are now world famous. Wilson's guests enjoyed concerts, one-act plays, and gourmet dinners cooked by European chefs. Wilson and his son now operate an art gallery on Red Arrow Highway. Devereux Bowly, a lawyer and writer from Chicago, purchased the inn in 1994 and conducted extensive renovation, including the addition of a restaurant. (Postcard courtesy of Robert Rosenbaum.)

This is the Shakespeare House, a replica of the home of Shakespeare, which served as the second clubhouse of the Chikaming Country Club. According to the *Centennial History of Lakeside*, Chikaming Country Club had been incorporated in 1912, with Jane Addams, famous founder of a Chicago settlement house, as its first member. The Chikaming Country Club dedicated the Shakespeare House and an 18-hole golf course in 1925. The American Meat Institute at the Livestock Exposition in Chicago had used the Shakespeare House before it was dismantled and reassembled in Lakeside. One of the gatherings held at the Shakespeare House was the annual meeting of a group of Chicago area scientists and physicians. Beginning in 1912, for about 10 years, Dr. A.J. Carlson hosted parties at his Harbert cottage for 10 or 12 scientists and physicians from the University of Chicago, where they held informal discussions. When joined by additional University of Chicago faculty and medical staff from Presbyterian/St. Luke's Hospital, they moved their meetings to the Chikaming Country Club. They met annually, except for the war year of 1917, until the 1970s. (Postcard courtesy of Robert Rosenbaum.)

Dr. George Larson and his wife Louisa operated the first resort in Lakeside at the turn of the century, charging $7 per week. Guests enjoyed nightly bonfires and marshmallow roasts on the beach. Larson also welcomed those who wished to get back to nature by living in tents, such as Dr. Holmes, a physician from Chicago, and his wife. Two University of Chicago professors, Myra Reynolds and Euphrosyne Langley, also put up a deluxe tent on property adjoining the Larson farm. The professors and the Holmeses eventually built cabins for themselves. Dr. Holmes used to come each weekend to join his wife by taking the boat to St. Joseph and riding his bicycle 20 miles to Lakeside. Early in the century there were seven resorts in Lakeside. Besides Larson's, they included: Pine Bluff Resort, built by Clarence Wilkinson in 1901; Orchard Beach; Aylesworth's Resort (which later became the Lakeside Inn); Shorewood, where Chicagoans purchased land and built summer cottages; Gottlieb's Grove; and Murphy's Grove. (Postcard courtesy of Robert Rosenbaum.)

Swedish Baptists from the south side of Chicago founded Bethany Beach in 1906 as a faith-based summer camp for needy children. At the Swedish Baptist Church's annual conference, they appointed three of their leaders, James Magnusen, G. Arvid Hagstrom, and Charles Palm, to find a desirable location for a summer camp. On April 12, 1905, they traveled to see a Sawyer farm that was advertised in the *Sunday Daily News*. They purchased the 40-acre fruit farm, platted it, and offered the lots for lease in church publications. They hoped that leasing land for summer homes would help finance the children's camp. However, lack of profit prevented this from happening at the time. Other investors, including Anton Noreen, were brought in. Within a few years, Noreen bought the property from the other investors and became the driving force behind the success of Bethany Beach. Because Bethany Beach was a faith-based community, one of the first buildings erected was the original tabernacle—in 1906. It was replaced by a new tabernacle in 1924, a structure which continues to serve the community today. The Swedish Baptist's Young Peoples' Union of Chicago conducted assemblies and held church services in the new tabernacle from 1924 to 1945. They used the slogan: "Eight Days Without a Dull Moment." Hundreds of young people attended each year. Besides church services, the young visitors participated in golf tournaments at the Bridgman golf course, ping-pong, horseshoes, horseback riding, swimming, tennis elimination tournaments, and concerts on Saturdays. Boys' and girls' camps were held from 1936 to 1945. Bethany Beach continues its tradition of maintaining a close-knit faith-based community, with many children and grandchildren of original visitors returning to enjoy summertime pleasures. Some of the original visitors have now settled in their beloved community on a full-time basis. (Postcard courtesy of Robert Rosenbaum.)

Guests of the River's Edge Bed and Breakfast in Union Pier return from an invigorating walk. Keith and Prudence Sindelar, current owners of the River's Edge on Community Hall Road in Union Pier, serve a delicious breakfast, including prize-winning muffins. Their 30 acres of land border the Galien River. They have apple, peach, and chestnut trees on their property, and canoeing and biking are available. Other bed and breakfasts in the Harbor Country area include Pine Garth, Sandpiper Inn, Garden Grove, the Inn at Union Pier, Pumpernickel, Gordon Beach, Garden Grove, White Rabbit, San Souci, Warren Woods, and Treasure House. Other Berrien County bed and breakfasts include Chestnut House, River Bend, South Cliff, and the Primrose Path. (Photo courtesy of Keith and Prudence Sindelar.)

This photo of Elm Street in downtown Three Oaks shows stores including RCA, Drier's Meat Market (which remains and is registered as a National Historic Landmark,) Rexall on the left, and the bowling alley, laundromat, and tavern on the right. Today Three Oaks has become a cultural magnet. It has art galleries, the Vicker's Theater, which shows art and vintage films, and the Acorn Theater, which has transformed part of the old Featherbone Factory to an attractive venue for theatrical and musical entertainment. (Photo courtesy of the Three Oaks Township Public Library.)

Early members of the Prairie Club pose in front of the Dewey Cannon in Three Oaks on June 4, 1910. Jens Jensen, seen here holding the flag, was a preeminent landscape architect who led many trips of the group to the Dunes. On the far left is H.C. Cowles, a prominent University of Chicago botanist and conservationist whose research traced the succession of plant life from the vegetation-less beach to the inland forest of maple. Also pictured is Henry J. Cox, a meteorologist and geographer. On the pedestal next to Jensen is Edward K. Warren, industrialist, philanthropist, and one of the founding fathers of Three Oaks, Michigan. The Prairie Club was organized in 1908 and incorporated in 1911. Its objective was to strengthen members' health, well-being, and appreciation of nature. Members hiked throughout Chicagoland and in the dunes and woods of Indiana and Michigan. They eventually established camps in Indiana (Tremont), Michigan (Hazelhurst), and Illinois (River Grove). The Prairie Club was also interested in conservation efforts, such as creating a National Park in the Indiana Dunes. Now a vital organization of 900 members, the club continues its outdoor activities and maintains the Hazelhurst and River Grove Camps. (Photo courtesy of the Prairie Club.)

Members of the Prairie Club gather in the woods, probably at Warren Woods in Three Oaks, in June of 1910. Warren Woods has one of the few remaining virgin beech-maple climax forests. The nonprofit Edward K. Warren Foundation gifted Warren Woods to the public, its first gift after the establishment of the foundation in 1917. The 311-acre tract, with more than 100 species of plants, is now a state park. The Warren Foundation also donated the land for the Warren Dunes on Lake Michigan in Sawyer, which also became a state park. (Photo courtesy of the Prairie Club.)

CASCADE ~ HIBBS' POND

LYTCHETT HOUSE

GREETINGS
FROM
HAZEL·HURST

The postcard shows four Hazelhurst summer cottages. After the sale of the Prairie Club's Tremont Camp in the Indiana Dunes to the Indiana Dunes State Park, the Prairie Club voted to purchase Hazelhurst Camp in Harbert. The camp, including a beach along Lake Michigan, was purchased from the estate of William R. Hibbs on February 1, 1930. Eleven structures existed when Hazelhurst was purchased. These included the Buena Vista Cottage, recently converted to a duplex which Prairie Club members can rent, and a barn which first served as the men's dormitory but is now a community center offering musical events, lectures about ecology, and meetings. After the sale of Tremont, Prairie Club moved 10 to 20 existing cottages to the Hazelhurst location. The club purchased other land and more cottages were built, so that now there are 94 site holders at the camp. Some of cottages have remained in the same family for many decades. (Postcard courtesy of Robert Rosenbaum.)

American poet Carl Sandburg cares for his wife's award-winning goats at their home at Birchwood in Harbert. Sandburg lived first in Tower Hill Highlands in Sawyer and then at Harbert's Birchwood Beach for about 15 years. Barbara Norby Cohen remembers him when he resided at Tower Hill Highlands. She says, "He used to sit on the beach, strum his guitar, and sing folk songs to us in a deep rapsy voice." While residing at Birchwood, Sandburg wrote his famous book on Abraham Lincoln. The award-winning goats his wife raised were shipped throughout the country. Some of Sandburg's neighbors objected to the smell of the goats. (Photo courtesy of the Three Oaks Township Public Library.)

This artful photo taken by R.E. Jackson at the turn of the century is cleverly labeled "Birchwood Bank Depositors in Line." In 1891, the original Birchwood property included beautiful beach land like this, as well as woods and a farm—a total of 80 acres. Wells Bradford Sizer purchased it from a widow in 1891, selling his bookstore in Chicago and moving his family into the home on the property. His parents joined him and farmed on the property. The Sizer family had many guests from Chicago, giving Wells the idea of building small cottages and renting them during the summer months. Later the cottages were individually owned; many of these have since been passed down from generation to generation. (Photo courtesy of Jack Sizer.)

In this R.E. Jackson photo, Birchwood Resort guests await a delicious meal to be served at the new Hemlock Dining Room, c. 1907. The guests did not have kitchens in their cottages. Many of the resorts offered the American plan, serving meals three times a day to their guests at a main dining area. Wells Sizer, who bought the property in 1881 and established the resort soon afterward, stands at the post; Larry Sizer, his son, sits on the bench in front. Larry Sizer recalls, "The whole family had to pitch in to help run the place." Larry remembers having to kill some 35 chickens each Saturday for Sunday dinner. He also had the awful chore, called "A Solemn Occasion," of emptying the outside toilets by dragging the tubs out onto a stone boat pulled by a horse and disposing of the contents in a prepared hole in or near the garden. (Photo courtesy of Jack Sizer.)

In the early part of the 20th century, fashion dictated that men wear skirts over their long swimming trunks. By 1920, women had shed much of their bulky swimwear but still wore leggings and slippers. Even in the 1890s, with all the bulky clothes, bathing at the beach was popular for men and women. The book *St. Joseph and Benton Harbor, The Twin Cities of the East Shore and Their Multitude of Attractions,* published in 1893, states: "There are three firms operating upward of 150 bath houses along the beach. These are supplied with conveniences for bathers at a small fee." Swimming was popular despite the fact that some religious institutions and even magazines like the *Ladies Home Journal* cautioned against the sexes swimming together (called "promiscuous" swimming). (Photo courtesy of Jack Sizer.)

Parties arranged by the management of the resort turned out to be a great hit with guests. In this photo, the participants of a Birchwood Resort party are dressed in white middies and crepe paper sailor hats. What fun! Hazel Sizer is fourth from the right and Larry Sizer is in the middle of the front row. (Photo courtesy of Jack Sizer.)

Some in this group seated on the deck of the Thomopoulos home in Dunewood in Bridgman have been visiting every summer for 25 years. Clockwise from left to right they are Peter Giannos, Peter Panos, George Bakos, Ada Stoes, Nick Thomopoulos, John Rassogianis, Kay Nikolaidou, Elaine Thomopoulos, Kiki Giannos, and Toni Panos. Whether you are a full-time resident or have a second home, if you have ties to Chicagoland, family or friends come to visit. Mike Economos vividly remembers the summer visitors who came to his family's second home in Stevensville. The home had a sleeping porch about thirty feet long with a lot of beds. Economos explains, "In those days, you never needed an invitation. Everybody was welcome."

Every day from Memorial Day to Labor Day, Corky Corliss and his wife Susan play taps to the setting of the sun at Weko Beach Park in Bridgman, with hundreds watching and listening with quiet contemplation. The playing of taps to commemorate the beautiful ending of the day at Weko Beach Park started in 1991. Weko Beach Park is named after Weber and Kohlander, partners who built the first beach house. Phyllis Weber, as quoted from the Bridgman Chamber of Commerce web page said, "People came from all over Chicago and South Bend in the early 1940s to eat some good German food and to dance. On Friday night they had fish frys. On Sundays, a group from the Chicago Symphony would come and give concerts." Going back to tradition, Bridgman now offers music on the beach every other Sunday during the summer. (Photo by Elaine Thomopoulos.)

These are three of the five original homes in Dunewood in Bridgman. From left to right, they are the Stracke, Krcilek, and Gouwens homes, built in the 1950s. The first residents of Dunewood, Natalie Y. Jordan and her two sons, went to realtor David Andreason for help in finding a summer home. Andreason had dreamed of developing the land but lacked the money. Jordan provided him with the funds for the first lot, although there was no access, survey, title, or deed. The lakefront lots and the lots adjacent to them sold quickly. Andreason also planned to develop land owned by the Bos-Hughes heirs. However, Andreason's death in 1967 left a vacuum, and the Dunewood community worried that the remaining land would be sold for sand mining. To prevent this, Jerry Mason, Dr. Gene Parker, and Horace Jordan formed a committee and established a corporation known as Dunewood II. During the summer of 1968, the members of Dunewood purchased 33 shares at $3,500 each, thus providing the funds to buy the tract. Stockholders drew for lots on August 28, 1979, deeds were issued, and the corporation was dissolved. All lots became a part of the Dunewood community. Another crisis arose in the early 1970s. There remained an unplatted tract in the Dunewood area, consisting of 30 beautifully wooded, hilly acres, owned by Earl Gray. The community organized, and following the procedure used in developing Dunewood II, a corporation was formed with Robert Dubois as president, Joe Johnson as vice president, and Louise Christensen as secretary-treasurer. Articles of incorporation were filed on May 17, 1976. When Gray died, his heirs had to be persuaded to sell the land. The Real Estate and Rules Committee, chaired by Leonard Grossman, carried out an ingenious plan for distributing the lots to the shareholders. Joe Johnson made a large plywood plat. Each person selected the lot he or she wanted and Grossman pinned the individual's name on the lot indicated. Then bidding started. After one person bid high enough to win the lot, the unsuccessful bidders could then move their names to other lots. The entire project was completed and the final plat was recorded on July 10, 1979. (Photo courtesy of Robert Gouwens.)

This is Winnick's Resort in Bridgman. (Postcard courtesy of Robert Rosenbaum.)

Emil Tosi, when interviewed by the Fort Miami Heritage Society in 1994, explained the development of Tosi's Resort and Restaurant in Stevensville. His parents immigrated to Cicero, Illinois, from the northern provinces of Italy. In 1922, they came to Stevensville. His mother bought 10 acres of land from the House of David for $10,000 and built a resort catering to the Italians from Cicero at the site of the present-day restaurant. Tosi said, "The main building we built was where the bar and dining room is now and we had about ten little cabins. Very Spartan. No indoor toilets, but they were only charged $17 per week! Then the restaurant started and my aunt and uncle were in with them. Then I came in a few years later. A little quirk about the Italians. When they first came in on a Sunday, they were heavy on the food. Then on Wednesday and Thursday they started taking Alka-Seltzer and cut down the rest of the week." In 1948, after his parents retired from the resort business, Tosi himself opened a small restaurant and bar that seated 35 to 50 guests. In 1960 he expanded and decorated it to make it look like an Italian Villa, with Italian sculptures, paintings, and an outdoor fountain. The fine dining restaurant, under different management, continues the tradition of culinary excellence that Emil Tosi started. (Photo courtesy of Fort Miami Heritage Society.)

According to the book *Stevensville and Area: 1884–1984*, Irwin and Katherine Rew, prominent members of the Evanston, Illinois, community, bought 35 acres of Stevensville property, comprised of dunes with oaks, maples, beech, and other hardwoods. They built this 16-room summer cottage mansion *c.* 1916; it featured 528 feet of beach frontage. They planted train carloads of Austrian Pine, Scotch pine, and Canadian hemlock. It took two men several weeks to plant the trees. Irwin Rew also maintained a Michigan fruit farm (called Bluffwood Farm). In 1958, Irwin's widow, Mrs. Katherine Rew, sold the property to Shag Sarkisian, who built the Snowflake Motel.

Stevensville's Snowflake Motel on Red Arrow Highway, with motel rooms spread out in a snowflake pattern around an interior courtyard, is listed on the National Registry of Historic Places. The majestically designed six-ton steel dome, silhouetted against the sky like a delicate snowflake, had a pool beneath. Originally there had been a huge 15-room summer "cottage" on the property, built by Irwin and Katherine Rew *c.* 1916. In 1958, after the mansion burned, Katherine Rew sold the property to Shag Sarkisian. He commissioned Frank Lloyd Wright to design the motel, but Wright died in 1959 before the drawings could be completed. However, Taliesin Associates of Spring Green, Wisconsin, an affiliate of the Frank Lloyd Wright Foundation, did complete the project. A Wright associate and Wright's son-in-law, Wesley Peters, prepared the working drawings. The motel, which opened in 1962, contained 57 rooms and a conference room with seating for up to 300 people. Pradyuman Patel, who now operates the motel, captures its unique design in his photographs. (Photo by Pradyuman Patel.)

The Dunham Grand Mere Resort, near the shore of Lake Michigan in Stevensville, had a main house with dining room and kitchen as well as a separate 11-room boarding house. Ella Dunham ran the resort. In 1910, her father, James, platted 14 acres into 60 lots, sold the lots for $50 to $75, and built several homes for his own family. Ella made one of these homes into a boarding house and a restaurant called the Old Homestead Tea Room. Grand Mere, now a state park, is a wondrous natural area of dunes, lakes, woods, and marsh, encompasses about 1,000 acres and borders the shore of Lake Michigan. It is part of a geologic formation called the Grand Marais embayment, which was formed by glaciers. There are three inland lakes in Grand Mere: North, Middle, and South. (Postcard courtesy of Fort Miami Heritage Society.)

Joseph and Tina Capozio established the La Conca D'oro Resort on Ridge Road in Stevensville in 1945. Their son, Gene, remembers it as a fun place where Sicilian Italians from Chicago came in summer. He says, "I never felt I needed to leave during the summer months, because everything you would ever want was in a two mile area: parties, beach, craziness. You never knew who was going to pull the biggest gag. One night my father ran out of wood for the bonfire. The guests started burning the chairs. He never ran out of wood again. Another time they rolled the jukebox out of the pizzeria at 3 a.m. and woke everybody up. There was musical stuff, with guitar or accordion. They would play poker or the slot machines." With his brother, Lenny, and their parents, Gene organized dances at the resort's tennis court near the beach. Gene remembers that disk jockeys from WLS flew their planes into the airport to perform at these dances, which attracted from 1,000 to 1,500 people between 1960 and 1963. In 1965 the resort closed, and the Capozio family built the Surfside Apartments on the land. Besides La Conca D'oro, other resorts serving Italians in the Ridge Road/Glenlord Road area included Tosi's, Clamar Court, Glenlord, Pisa, Foreani, and Carmaniagni. (Photo courtesy of Capozio's.)

Fran Poulos Katsaros and her family and friends spend a sunny day at the beach *c.* 1945. The family stayed at the Sunset View Cottages north of Benton Harbor year after year. "Like a little Greek town," is how her brother Nick Poulos (Panagopoulos) describes the resort where he vacationed during the 1930s and 1940s. He remembers the *parea* (companionship) of other Greek families and the singing of Greek songs, such as "To Gelekaki Pou Fores (The Vest You Wear)," played with the accompaniment of an accordion. Greeks who spent summers in Southwest Michigan banded together to recreate the idyllic rural type of lifestyle they left behind in Greece. Aphrodite Demeur, a native of Greece, noted, "It was like going back to the homeland." (Photo courtesy of Fran Katsaros.)

Lou Pazoles cooks in his family's rented cottage, *c.* 1948. He used to stay at the Sunset View near Hagar Shores with his family. (Photo courtesy of Fran Katsaros.)

John Higman developed Higman Park in St. Joseph *c.* 1900. Olaf Benson, landscape gardener and designer, designed the grounds. Higman offered L.L. Gap Cottage Sites for sale. They included 146 acres, with one acre of lakefront. He advertised, "River and Lake for boating and fishing, fine ground for camping, wooded ravines, hillside and table lands for picnics, together with apple, pear and peach orchards, vineyards and small fruit combine to make a park unequaled for natural beauty. Your choice of lots in these additions: Higman Lake Bluff Park, Pokagon Heights, or Perfections Beach. Strictest care will be taken to protect purchase and keep out all objectionable features. John Higman, Jr. Owner, St. Jo. Mich." (Postcard courtesy of Fort Miami Heritage Society.)

This postcard is of the Higman Park Lagoon. *Metropolis of the Fruit Belt*, a book published in 1915, calls Higman Park "The Gem of All Resorts." It certainly sounds like that from the advertisement, "The cottages are modern and equipped for housekeeping, having running water, both hot and cold, bath rooms, open fire places, large verandas and well kept lawns. . . . Its chicken and fish dinners are famous. The fruits and vegetables served on its tables are grown especially for the Inn. The milk supply is from special cows." Guests were transported there via the Pere Marquette or Michigan Central Railroads and the Graham and Morton steamships. (Postcard courtesy of Fort Miami Heritage Society.)

The car in this photo bears the words "Higman Park Villa." The original hotel at Higman Park in Benton Harbor was a three-story frame building called the Higman Park Inn. It was built c. 1900 and was destroyed by fire in 1913, when 25 guests were forced to flee the hotel. After the fire, the Pavilion on the Lake was expanded and became the hotel. The pavilion had recreation and bathing facilities and a pier. A launch brought passengers from the Graham and Morton Dock to this pier. To facilitate water travel to the park, a canal was built from the nearest loop of the Paw Paw River to a place near the road which ended at the beach and Pavilion. An alternate means of travel was provided by a horse-drawn bus which made the trip from the city boat dock to the park. (Photo courtesy of the Benton Harbor Public Library.)

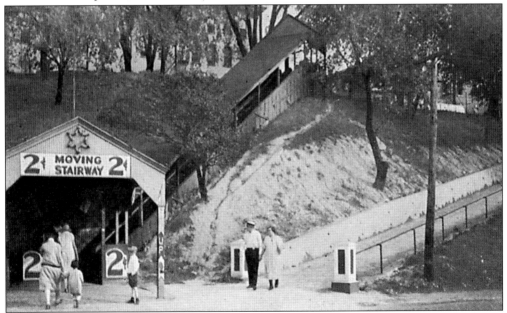

For a fee of 2¢, people could to ride the moving stairway up the bluff of Lake Bluff Park rather than walk. (Postcard courtesy of Dick Grau.)

This postcard, dated August 21, 1911 and sent to Chicago, shows the harbor and steamship docks of St. Joseph. In the left background is the airplane ride from Silver Beach. The pleasures of traveling on Graham and Morton steamships were extolled in the book *Echoes of Summer Time Pleasures*, published in 1893. The volume tried to persuade travelers who had come to see the Columbia Exposition to stay in St. Joseph by using this persuasive argument, "You have traveled by rail in the summer? Yes, of course. Well the less said about it the better—But a trip on a commodious and elegantly appointed steamer is happily a different thing. . . . The airy roominess and purity of all about breathing a freedom broader, deeper, grander than ever dreamed of. . . . Can you afford to enjoy these delightful trips across the lake? Rather ask, can you afford to forego them, since they will be cheaper than for you to remain in the hot and crowded city?" (Postcard courtesy of Fort Miami Heritage Society.)

People on vacation enjoyed walking in Lake Bluff Park, a park donated to the city of St. Joseph by Junius Hatch. The book *Heart of the Fruit Belt* states that in 1897, over 250,000 visitors to St. Joseph stayed at the local hotels and boarding houses. This did not include 115,000 who arrived and departed the same day, nor 800 or more full-time summer residents. (Photo courtesy of Fort Miami Heritage Society.)

This dog looks out at the harbor, with Plank's Tavern (renamed Hotel St. Joseph) in the background. Steamers coming from Chicago landed patrons right on the hotel grounds. Trains also stopped at the station on the grounds. An 1889 newspaper article compared the hotel favorably to Planks' Grand Hotel at Mackinac Island. A massive structure of 40 to 80 feet on the side and 420 feet long, it also had a 400-foot balcony. Because the hotel had its own heating and lighting plant and its own waterworks, it was completely self-sufficient. The amenities included a dancing pavilion, a ladies' writing room with a velvet carpet, a gentlemen's writing room, a gentlemen's smoking room and reading room, a reception room for ladies, several dining halls, a dancing hall, a breakfast room, and eight to ten other rooms for receptions. Tragically, this magnificent hotel burned down in 1898. According to a *Daily Palladium* article, the bellboy and bartender shouted "Fire!" and pounded on doors. The article went on to say, "Everyone at once began to call loudly and soon the frightened guests hastily or partially dressed were pouring through the building. . . . While guests were aroused one lady was discovered in her room without a stitch of clothing on her person except her shoes, which she was deliberately lacing, seeming to be bewildered. The employee who found her helped her to dress and get out of the building." Altogether 40 guests and 50 employees escaped and one employee died. The massive frame structure burned quickly, and the St. Joseph fire engine could not get across the river. According to the newspaper article, "An attempt was made while the fire was raging to get the St. Joseph fire engine across the river. It was taken to the Graham dock but before means had been provided to get it over it was found to be of no avail, as other buildings threatened were then out of danger." The shivering guests made their way across the river in boats and found lodging in hotels and residents' homes.

In the January 27, 1966 issue of the *News-Palladium*, Luton Wyman recalled the old St. Joseph train depot as it was *c.* 1910 before this newer one was built. He said that the old depot was divided into two rooms, one for men and one for women, with a small ticket office in between. Potbelly stoves kept each room warm. He remarks, "There was soft coal, dirty spittoons and mud on the wooden floor, tracked in from outside for there were no sidewalks. An old leaky water hydrant outside was the only place one could get a drink or wash one's hands. There were not so many cigarette smokers in those days but there were plenty of pipe smokers and those that chewed tobacco. What a mess around those old dirty stoves!" Amtrak continues to provide service to the St. Joseph station. (Photo courtesy of Fort Miami Heritage Society.)

Edgewater Club, St. Joseph, Mich.

The Edgewater Club House in St. Joseph is pictured on this postcard dated July 1919. The Edgewater Club, a large resort with a 440-foot veranda, was built in 1909. Fire consumed it in 1931. An annex, built *c.* 1911, still survives. (Postcard courtesy of Dick Grau.)

This photo shows the dedication of Benton Harbor's Jean Klock Park in 1917. After the voters of Benton Harbor rejected a proposal to buy the parcel, J.N. and Carrie Klock bought the half-mile of lakefront and 90 acres of land and donated it to the city. They named it Jean Klock Park in memory of their daughter, who died when she was an infant. (Photo courtesy of Fort Miami Heritage Society.)

The Michigan Hotel was located at Territorial and Water in Benton Harbor. You can also see Nick's Lunch and Billiards. In 1928, the Michigan Hotel was built by brothers Nick and John Dorotheon and their cousin, Alex Gust, immigrants from the island of Samos in Greece. By 1929, George Andrews, John's son-in-law, also became involved in running the hotel. The 45-room hotel became noted for the Shangri-La Bar and the elegant Palm Garden Restaurant on the roof. (Photo courtesy of Fort Miami Heritage Society.)

Echoes of Summer Time Pleasures, published in 1893, describes the joy of fishing at the turn of the century: "Every body likes to fish. That is, of course, if they can catch anything—and at St. Joseph everybody can catch fish. It's a universal pastime, enjoyed by all classes. It is a common sight to see from fifty to a hundred boats at the mouth of the river, and twice that number of persons along the piers and docks. . . . Immense quantities [of fish] are thus taken daily, but with the vast resources of Lake Michigan to draw from, the supply is never diminished. Cisco, perch, pickerel, bass of several varieties, and the ubiquitous bull head are the principal kinds taken, although in some interior streams the wary speckled trout can be lured. St. Joseph harbor is one of the few places on the Great Lakes where that prince of game fish, the white bass, can be caught. At seasons when they bite freely, the harbor presents a most animated appearance, the exciting sport sometimes extending far into the night." (Photo courtesy of Fort Miami Heritage Society.)

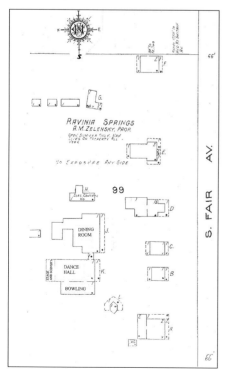

Zelensky's Ravinia Springs Resort on Fair Avenue in Benton Harbor had a dining hall, bowling alley, dance hall, and stage; the various types of buildings are shown on this 1928 Sanborn's Insurance Map. An article in the August 18, 1909 issue of the *News-Palladium* tells this heart-rending story, "Jew and Gentile opened their purse at the benefit entertainment at Zelensky's resort last evening, and when the evening's program was over a fund of $1,000 had been raised for the benefit of the Marks Nathan Jewish Orphan Home of Chicago. In the big amusement hall, a program was rendered by members of the home, orphan children, ranging in ages from 6 to 12 years. A child of six, Doran Omansky, moved the big audience to tears when she sang, 'Which Way Did Mama Go?' Long before the child had finished her song a downpour of money began to flood the state. In the words the sweet-faced singer rendered, the audience recognized a pathetic appeal for the home which was sheltering the tot, and Jew and Gentile rivaled one another in showering the little one with money."

This image shows St. Joseph's south pier with the lighthouse and a steamship in the background.

Tourists and locals alike enjoyed food and drink at the Lion's Saloon on 196 Water Street in Benton Harbor. The saloon, which overlooked the canal, was operated by two immigrants from Greece, Tom State and Peter Bizanes. In the 1930s, Bizanes also had a beer garden and concession stand at Silver Beach. Today one of the local taverns in Benton Harbor is owned by the son of a Greek immigrant, "Babe" Couvelis. He has been operating this business, on Riverview Drive near the St. Joseph River, since 1975, and has had a bar in Benton Harbor since 1957. He and his brother Steve started working at their parents' business in the 1940s. (Postcard courtesy of Benton Harbor Public Library.)

This is "four corners" in Benton Harbor, with the Hotel Benton to the left, located on the northeast corner of Main and Water Streets. The Hotel Benton was built in 1890 by Edward Brant, who earned great wealth in the lumber business. In 1941, the western portion of the building was razed, and in 1987 the entire structure was destroyed by fire. This revitalized area is now known as the Arts District. (Photo courtesy of Fort Miami Heritage Society.)

The Whitcomb (formerly the St. Charles) and the Lake View Hotels are shown on the bluff in St. Joseph in this 1896 photo. The Maids of the Mist fountain is in front of the Whitcomb. In 1928, the old Whitcomb Hotel was torn down to make way for the current structure. The Whitcomb stopped functioning as a hotel in 1966 and the building now serves as a retirement residence. (Photo courtesy of Fort Miami Heritage Society.)

Vacationers enjoyed going to the theaters, first for vaudeville and silent films and then for talkies. This photograph shows advertising for two theaters, the Bijou Princess and the Liberty in Benton Harbor. The Liberty was showing a double feature: "My American Wife" starring Gloria Swanson along with "Nanook of the North." The Bijou was built in 1906, and the Liberty in 1922. Sadly, both theaters are now gone. The only theater remaining is the State Theater. (Photo courtesy of Fort Miami Heritage Society.)

This unique postcard of Whitcomb Sulphur Springs Hotel in St. Joseph shows the heated swimming pool. The advertisement reads, "Michigan's outstanding hotel and health spa in the heart of the fruit belt." Another hotel attraction was Polly the Parrot, sitting on her perch outside the aviary. Local resident Betty Hunt recalls, "She shocked guests with swear words like, 'Damn it, Shut that Door!'" Hunt also remembers seeing the Whitcomb's summer guests sitting outside in their chaise lounges. (Postcard courtesy of Fort Miami Heritage Society.)

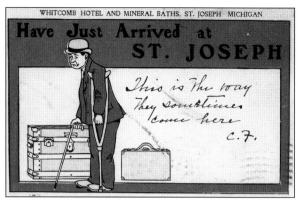

These cartoons by Longstaff, printed in 1905, illustrate the wondrous powers attributed to the mineral baths at the Whitcomb Hotel. James Tatooles remembers, "The hotel just stunk of this stuff, high humidity. It was just a horrible kind of a place for us kids. But somehow or other the adults thought it was therapeutic. And they would always go there as a low class spa, I would call it." Other hotels with mineral baths included the Premier, Dwan, and Salzman in Benton Harbor. The baths were very important to the commerce of the city, as noted in the following slogan found in book published by the Benton Harbor Chamber of Commerce in 1915, "On to a Hundred Thousand Bathers a Year." By the 1950s the baths had declined, and today not even one bath remains. (Postcards courtesy of Fort Miami Heritage Society.)

This advertisement ran in the *Chicago Evening Post* on June 22, 1922. To lure people to take subscriptions, the newspaper offered lots near the shores of Lake Michigan, north of Benton Harbor, for $54.50. This area, Lake Michigan Beach in Hagar Shores, continues to be a second-home community and many current residents are descendants of those who bought the lots through the *Chicago Evening Post* ad.

Two

RESORTS NEAR THE INLAND LAKES, RIVERS, AND COUNTRYSIDE

The Crystal Palace remains a romantic legend, where many couples met, fell in love, and got married. The Crystal Palace had a rough beginning. One week before the dance pavilion on Paw Paw Lake was to open, it burned down. Much to everyone's amazement, a rebuilt ballroom opened about six weeks later, on May 30, 1925. Both summer visitors and local residents throughout Berrien County used to enjoy the dancing on the 120-by-220-foot floor. The Crystal Palace ballroom was built by Frank Dlouhy, a Chicago homebuilder, and his brother-in-law, Richard Macek. Two generations of the Dlouhy family operated it. It was sold in 1962 and burned to the ground in 1963. Nothing but lovely memories remain. (Postcard courtesy of Fort Miami Heritage Society.)

CRYSTAL PALACE

Paw Paw Lake, Coloma, Mich.

presents

The Big Beat

of

Buddy Morrow

and his orchestra

Saturday, Sept. 3rd

Adm. $1.75 per person — Tax Included

These cards were mailed out to 1,500 prospective patrons of the Crystal Palace in Paw Paw Lake. Note the admission price of $1.75. The ballroom accommodated as many as 2,000 people. Big name entertainers like Louis Armstrong, Perry Como, Doris Day, Les Brown, Tommy Dorsey, Jimmy Dorsey, Guy Lombardo, Stan Kenton, Hal Kemp, Tommy Mercer, Harry James, Glenn Miller, and Merv Griffin performed there. Dancers also enjoyed the music of local bands, such as Bob Lewis. (Postcard courtesy of Benton Harbor Public Library.)

COTTAGES - STRONG'S RESORT, PAW PAW LAKE, COLOMA, MICHIGAN   87789

Bathers enjoy Strong's Landing. The Strong Farm Home opened in 1888, after George Strong enlarged his farm so that he could take in boarders. He later built cottages.

Rick Rasmussen's great-grandparents, August and Helen Bowman, and a friend stand in front of their summer cottage called Wildwood on Paw Paw Lake. The postcard's greeting, written in Old Swedish, noted the great fishing and good times the writer was having. Rasmussen found the postcard at an event that featured over a half million postcards at 150 tables. He recalls: "After hours of looking and finding six postcards relating to Paw Paw Lake, I headed for the front door. I decided to stop at one last dealer. While looking through his Michigan cards I paused and gave cry of delight. There in my hands was a postcard connecting me to my own family history at Paw Paw Lake. After 88 years, this card has found its way back home to a place of honor." Rasmussen is the author of several excellent books on the Paw Paw Lakes and now resides at Paw Paw Lake full-time. (Photo postcard courtesy of Rick Rasmussen.)

The steamboat *Gypsy* on Paw Paw Lake, c. 1897, announces the dancing at Birchwood. Captain Feltus owned the *Gypsy*, said to be the fastest boat on Paw Paw Lake at that time. (Postcard courtesy of Dick Grau.)

This postcard of the Whip-Por-Will Hotel on Little Paw Paw Lake was sent to Chicago in 1909. Beginning at the turn of the century, many Chicagoans and Hoosiers vacationed at the boarding houses and resort hotels of Paw Paw Lake and Little Paw Paw Lake, and some enjoyed themselves so much that they bought second homes. Some of those who established second homes have now permanently settled in the area, a phenomenon throughout Berrien County. (Postcard courtesy of Benton Harbor Public Library.)

This postcard shows Rick Rasmussen's grandmother and grandfather, Lillian Bowman (second row, in a white blouse) and Louis Rasmussen (beside her, in a dark jacket), at Paw Paw Lake in 1910. You can tell Louis is smitten with Lillian; he has his hand around her waist. On the table sits the First Place trophy that Lou won when he raced his boss's boat in a Paw Paw Lake race. Lou's boss, Mr. Lungstrom, owned a summer cottage in Paw Paw Lake and so did Lillian's parents. Lillian and Louis got married a couple of years after this photo was taken. (Photo postcard courtesy of Rick Rasmussen.)

Couples enjoy refreshments in the Woodward Pavilion at Paw Paw Lake. Note the souvenirs and postcards in the foreground. Snow collapsed the first Pavilion in January of 1910, but by the summer it was rebuilt. In 1940, the pavilion was converted into a bowling alley, and later it was moved back from the lake. Unfortunately, fire destroyed it in 1949. According to the book *Trails from Shingle Diggin's*, Mrs. and Mrs. Orrin Woodward began welcoming guests to their home in 1890. They built the pavilion on piles over the water and also built a hotel which could accommodate 250 guests. (Postcard courtesy of Benton Harbor Public Library.)

This postcard, postmarked 1930, pictures "The new Woodward Pavilion on the Coloma side of Paw Paw Lake." Other pavilions on Paw Paw Lake included the Birchwood and Forest Beach Pavilions on the Watervliet side of the lake, as well as Edgewater Pavilion. Ray Kroc, who played piano at the Edgewater in 1919, met his first wife, Ethel Flemming, there. Her parents owned the May-Bell Hotel at Lakewood Point. Kroc went on to found McDonald's. In his book, *A History of Paw Paw Lake, Michigan*, Rick Rasmussen writes that Kroc and the band played tunes on one of the boats while cruising on shore. One of the members stood in the bow calling out, "Dance tonight at the Edgewater. Don't miss out on the fun." (Postcard courtesy of Benton Harbor Public Library.)

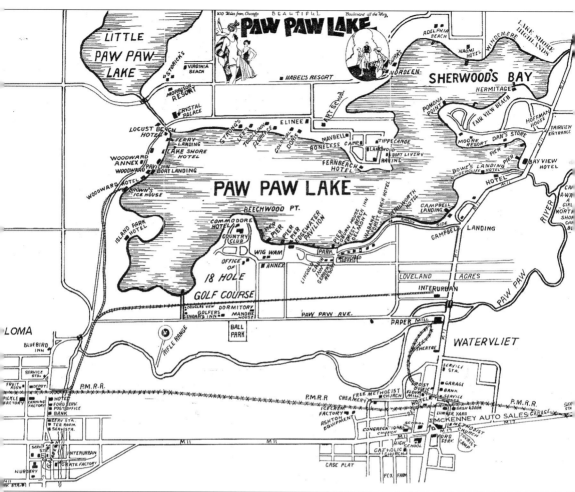

This 1930s map of the Paw Paw Lakes area shows the various resorts. The two lakes bordered both Coloma and Watervliet. Paw Paw Lake's resort culture began *c.* 1890, when Dr. Wakeman Ryno exchanged his village property for a part of J.H. Jones' farm, which became know as the Wil-O-Paw area. An advertisement in the *Berrien County Directory* of 1896 reads: "With its pure water, pure milk and butter, fine fishing, sailing, and bathing, this resort needs only to investigated to be appreciated. Having opened this location for cottages, will lease lot, or rent cottage by the week or for the season, on the reasonable terms. For further particulars, address Wakeman Ryno, M.D." Transportation to the Paw Paw Lakes resort area helped in the development of the resort business. Dr. William Baker's steam engine ran from Coloma to Paw Paw Lake. On July 4, 1896, a big celebration of the railroad's arrival attracted 5,000 people. The celebration included a troop of the Black Hussar Squadron from Chicago with 120 horses, 56 uniformed men, and 22 ladies. According to Mrs. A.C. Stark in her 1959 article in the *Courier*, Baker's railroad was credited with carrying 15,000 passengers the first season. In 1903, Baker began building an electric railway line from Benton Harbor to Paw Paw Lake via Coloma. However, the Benton Harbor-St. Joseph Railway Company built their own interurban electric railway, curtailing Baker's plans. When the interurban stopped coming to Coloma in 1920, buses ran from Benton Harbor. (Map courtesy of Rick Rasmussen.)

This Paw Paw Lake brochure lists the various activities available to visitors. (Brochure courtesy of the North Berrien Historical Society.)

The Ellinee Social Center on the Coloma side of Paw Paw Lake became a popular gathering place. It started as a modest store selling groceries and souvenirs in the early 1900s. Through the years it added a gas station, a bar and dance floor, an ice cream parlor, an arcade, and boxball alleys. Ernest H. Erickson, his wife Hildegard, and Dorothy and Frene, their daughters, ran the Ellinee. In 1971 the Ellinee closed and was torn down shortly afterwards. In the years prior to World War I, there were 50 resort hotels around Paw Paw Lake. During the depression and World War II, the number of resorters declined. Gasoline rationing made it difficult to travel during the war. After the war, in the 1950s and 1960s, vacationers took advantage of improved cars and roads, as well as travel by plane, to venture to other areas. By 1960 the resorts and motels had lost business and by 1993, only two remained.

In this image, swimmers enjoy Spink's Spring Bluff Resort, c. 1898. The resort was located about two miles from St. Joseph. As early as the 1860s, vacationers ventured to southwestern Michigan. According to an unpublished paper by John Spink, in the middle 1860s Robert Spink started his resort near the bluff on Spring Bluff Road, overlooking the river near what is now the end of May Street. The Spink family operated the resort until 1896, when it was sold. The land on which the resort was situated originally belonged to Robert's father, Samuel Spink, who came from New York. Robert purchased 68 acres of his father's farm, including Spink's Island. As well as growing fruit, he founded the resort, which accommodated 80 people. Spinks picked up his guests at St. Joseph or Benton Harbor from the boat or train with a team of horses and his buggy. At the resort they enjoyed the beauty of the St. Joseph River and surrounding orchards. Resorters took pleasure in hiking, boating, fishing, swimming, and a water slide down the bluff, as well as the fresh fruit from the farm. (Photo courtesy of Fort Miami Heritage Society.)

This postcard of the Emery Resort, located on the St. Joseph River at the dead end of Jakway Drive in Fairplain, is postmarked October 1909. The 1906 *St. Joseph City Directory* reported that the Emery Fruit Farm Resort was located on "50 acres of the best fruit land." The advertisement describes the view from the tower, "From where is seen the twin cities of St. Joseph and Benton Harbor to the north, the river winding in and out among the hills, forming a picture pen nor brush can paint. . . . Just in front the home in midstream is a beautiful wooded island belonging to the farm. This in itself is an artist's inspiration." From the 1920s to the 1950s the resort was owned consecutively by Nick Manglaris, James Douvas, and George Davros. It became a lively summer gathering place for the Greeks of Chicago and Gary, with Greek dancing, singing, late-night card games and delicious Greek food. (Postcard courtesy of Fort Miami Heritage Society.)

The *May Graham* became a beloved part of Berrien County lore, transporting passengers for a delightful ride down the St. Joseph River all the way to Berrien Springs from 1878 to 1908. The rotund and jovial Captain James Fikes and his wife, Caroline, took very good care of the passengers. Traveling on the riverboats like the *May Graham* was a relaxing way to spend a summer afternoon. An advertisement notes that, "It goes up the winding stream for 25 miles stopping at a score of landings, each of which seems more delightful than all the others for a day's picnic." The interurban eventually replaced the *May Graham* and she spent her last years in Grand Haven. (Photo courtesy of Fort Miami Heritage Society.)

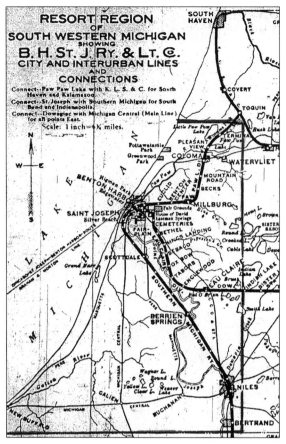

The interurban became an important link in traveling to the various attractions in St. Joseph and Benton Harbor, to the farm resorts on the river, and to the Paw Paw Lakes area. Note the stops at the various resorts (e.g., Sebago, Ox Bow, Tabors). By transferring to another train, a traveler could arrive from South Haven, Kalamazoo, or South Bend. With the advent of the interurban and the automobile, the boats that traveled up and down the rivers lost their business. On this map, Berrien County's borders are indicated with the three straight lines which meet each other at 90 degree angles. (Image courtesy of the Benton Harbor Public Library.)

This horse-drawn streetcar transported passengers through St. Joseph and Benton Harbor. In 1885, Murwin C. Barnes built the first street railway between the twin cities. It had four horse-drawn cars, each pulled by two horses. It traveled between Elm and State Steets in St. Joseph and Main and Pipestone Streets in Benton Harbor. Colonel W. Worth Bean purchased the horse-drawn line and by 1892 he had the first electric trolley in operation. (Photo courtesy of Fort Miami Heritage Society.)

A Southern Michigan Railway Co. interurban traveled on the largest interurban bridge in the world, located in Berrien Springs. The interurban bridge was completed December 1, 1905, and was 1,600 feet in length. The interurban service to Berrien Springs was discontinued at midnight on June 2, 1934. (Photo courtesy of Fort Miami Heritage Society.)

The dam created Lake Chapin in Berrien Springs, a lake enjoyed by many summer visitors. In 1908, many people came out to celebrate the completion of the I&M dam, built so that electricity could be generated. Lake Chapin was named to honor Henry Chapin, a native of Niles and a major stockholder. (Photo courtesy of Fort Miami Heritage Society.)

The Sebago Resort in Sodus on the St. Joseph River (about eight miles from St. Joseph and Benton Harbor), opened in 1895, with John J. Theis of Chicago as the proprietor. The *St. Joseph City Directory* of 1896 says that it opened with accommodations for 60 guests, with plans to add more cottages. The resort, like others in this area, offered a roomy hall for dancing, tennis courts, croquet grounds, a baseball diamond and "provision for outdoor sports to suit all." The guests could use boats for fishing and enjoyed swimming in the river where there were "deep, dandy bottom pools, with just enough current to keep them continually fresh; great trees overhead provide shade, enabling bather to disport themselves without exposure to a scorching sun." A unique attraction was the waterslide. A "hidden" attraction becomes apparent in the article written for the *Benton Harbor News Palladium* in 1918. "Last night the Sebago Resort in Sodus Township was successfully raided and a goodly amount of whiskey taken as evidence. Huge amounts of empty whiskey bottles recently attracted the attention of several Sodus township folk and complaints began to be handed in to the sheriff's office, with the result of the place being raided yesterday. Under the new state ruling on the 'bone dry' laws it is permissible for officials to search every room in either a public or a private resort. This was done, although the proprietor stoutly affirmed that no booze was held on the premises. Investigation, however, disclosed the fact that in several 'guest' rooms half pints of the fiery liquid were stored. In the private room of the owner the greater part of a one quart bottle of Rock and Rye was confiscated as evidence." (Postcard courtesy of Floyd and Donna Jerdon.)

This photo of Ox Bow Bend in the St. Joseph River, near Tabor Farm opposite the intersection of Ox Bow Road and River Road in Sodus, was taken in 1896. The farmers located along the rivers often would convert rooms of their home or build cottages to accommodate the onslaught of tourists, finding that it brought more income than farming. (Photo courtesy of Fort Miami Heritage Society.)

Who are the unidentified people in this vintage photo? By the way they are dressed, they appear to be a farmer, his wife, and tourists. Many of the farmers along the river took in summer boarders. Note the distinguished attire worn by the men in the boats. (Photo courtesy of Fort Miami Heritage Society.)

Elizabeth Jane Gray Manley and Edwin H. Manley bought the Langley home in St. Joseph in order to accommodate resort guests. According to Jane Granzow Miles, the Manleys' granddaughter, the 10 acres near the St. Joseph River included remnants of the Burnett apple orchard, planted by trader William Burnett's son, Frank. The home bought by the Manleys was the second Langley home built on the property; fire consumed the first. The family moved into the home c. 1908. Frank Langley, son of Captain and Mrs. Langley, lived there until his death. Miles has explained that the Manleys got started in the resort business quite by accident, when a vacationer came knocking, having heard of Mrs. Manley's extraordinary pie. (Photo courtesy of Jane Granzow Miles.)

Guests pose with their children during the early years of the Manleys' Myrtle Banks Resort, in the 1910s. The resort's name came from the myrtle that grew on the riverside property. Jane Miles' grandfather, a Canadian immigrant, farmed the adjacent land until he died in 1928, supplying produce for the resort. According to Miles, Grandpa Manley always seemed to be dressed up, wearing a white shirt and a tie, even while farming. The first guests at the Manleys' resort were Jewish and the resort business grew when visitors recommended it to their friends and relatives. (Photo courtesy of Jane Granzow Miles.)

Catherine Granzow, owner of the Manley Resort, took this photo of Manley Resort guests in 1948, with the Kodak camera she received for her high school graduation in 1918. Jane Miles, her daughter, reminisces about the women in the photo, "They went through my mother's pregnancy with her, and when I was born, they gave me gifts. I remember Auntie May LaChrone gave me a pretty little teapot that I have today. It was a tight, friendly group. When we attended the symphony in Chicago, we stayed with the Siegel family. Violet and Irving Jacobson visited throughout the year." (Photo courtesy of Jane Granzow Miles.)

Guests pose with the owner of the Manley Resort, Catherine Granzow. Jane Miles, Granzow's daughter, remembers the guests asking her mother to join the group for this photo. Catherine was the only one of four children who chose to stay and be a part of running the resort. When the resort first opened, Miles' grandparents, Elizabeth Jane Gray Manley and Edwin H. Manley, operated the resort. Edwin, a pharmacist as well as a farmer, sold patent medicine, using photos of his children on the labels. After Edwin died, Miles' grandmother and her mother and father, Catherine and John Granzow, ran the resort. (Photo courtesy of Jane Granzow Miles.)

These pretty local girls served as waitresses at the Manley Resort in 1949. They are, from left to right: Marilyn Hahn Gersonde, Dorie Lou Boonstra Gast, Sally Kesterke Petzke, and Jane Granzow Miles. The resort served three meals every day, except Sunday, so the waitresses worked hard. Jane started waiting tables when she was 13 years old. But even as a little girl she helped out at the resort. "When I was very young I helped by handing up clothespins to whomever was hanging up clothes, emptying wastebaskets, killing flies, shucking corn, shelling peas, snapping beans, drying dishes, picking flowers, whatever a little kid could do." When there were too many guests during the summer, Jane gave up her bed and slept on a cot in the living room. This was similar to the experiences of other children whose parents owned resorts. Miles recalls, "There were many pluses and minuses to growing up in the resort business. It was hard work, but I don't think my parents ever regretted it. I still miss the resort. It was my second home. I have many wonderful memories. It was a close-knit group. If one person went to the beach it was, 'Come everyone, pile in the car and we'll all go to the beach.' I grew up with the kids in the resort. If they went to the beach, I was always included. Many of the little mementos at the house were given to me by women who came to the resort every summer. I was born in August so they went through my mother's pregnancy [with her]. Many of the women that I grew up with I called 'aunt.' They were like aunts, like a family to me. I just can't explain what a close-knit group of people [we were]." (Photo courtesy of Jane Granzow Miles.)

Manley Resort guests pose for a photo in 1946. The Manley Resort served four generations until it closed in 1954 because guests started going to Florida and other locales. Jane Miles, who grew up at the resort, reports, "There were never any planned activities. [Visitors] planned their own fun. In the early days they swam in the river. It was clean then. There were several boats to use. They played baseball, croquet, whatever games were popular. They went to Silver Beach, to the movies, the House of David, to town to shop. Sometimes some of the men would go fishing. They played cards, read, and just plain relaxed. I can remember there was always a game of Monopoly going on, on one of the screened-in porches. And woe to the little kid who messed up the game as it usually went on for several days. The little kids played hide and seek, statue, and kick the can. The women loved to play mahjongg. I can still see their red fingernails moving the pieces and hear the soft click of those ivory tiles as they bumped together. This game was so foreign to me with the strange writing on the tiles." At the Manley Resort, as in other resorts in the 1930s, 1940s, and 1950s, children spent hour after hour without adult supervision, making up and playing their own games, wandering the beach and the countryside. Vaso Powers sums up why the free time she had as a child while on vacation in Michigan made a difference. "It was a very unstructured time in contrast to school and teachers telling you what to do. I think that unstructured time is really important for people to have as they're growing up. You get some sense of yourself and what you like. You need to work through your own head and figure out who you are." (Photo courtesy of Jane Granzow Miles.)

The inscription on the back of this photo reads: "Boy and girl meet at Tabor Farm in Sodus." Hundreds of young people who visited resort communities such as Grand Beach, Bethany Beach, and Paw Paw Lake formed romantic attachments, many of which led to marriage. Some of the young visitors from Chicago and Indiana wed local boys or girls, who followed their spouses out of the area. Yet other out-of-towners moved to Berrien County to be with their new mates. Herb Hahn, from Benton Harbor, met Elizabeth Koutas, from Hammond, Indiana, while she vacationed in St. Joseph with her parents. Herb recalls, "Every year she'd come into town, I'd bump into her someplace, at Silver Beach, Shadowland, Crystal Palace, or Tip-Top Café." After they married, Elizabeth moved to Benton Harbor where they raised their children, Lynette and Jim. Margie Andrews, a Benton Harbor native, met her husband, George Souliotis of Chicago, while he vacationed at the Manglaris Resort (formerly the Emery Fruit Farm Resort). Within one year, they were married. After spending five years in Chicago they moved to Benton Harbor, where they raised their children, George and Mary. (Photo courtesy of Fort Miami Heritage Society.)

This vintage photo shows Tabor Farm Resort, in Sodus, in the 1910s. In 1854, Wallace Tabor began growing fruit on this property. By the early 1890s, his son, Ernest Tabor, established the resort on a bluff overlooking the tranquil St. Joseph River. Located on 160 acres, with abundant fruit, it attracted thousands of visitors for more than 75 years. Joe Bachunas bought the farm from Tabor in the 1920s. Bachunas' brother, Al, later joined him as a partner. Another brother, Walter, also came to help. The brothers, with their wives Marie, Sophia, and Helen, along with Al's children, Ted and Elaine, worked hard seven days a week from spring through fall to maintain the resort. Until after World War II, it was a working farm with guinea hens, chickens, and horses. (Photo courtesy of the Bachunas Trust.)

Ted Bachunas sums up Tabor Farm Resort, "What made the place were the guests. They were terrific!" At Tabor Farm, activities were scheduled for each day of the week, but the guests made all the arrangements for the activities; these included staff and guest talent shows, shuffleboard, "crazy golf" (pictured), and a sing-a-long. In those days, things were more leisurely. Guests spent hours of unscheduled time just talking, playing board games, cards, horseshoes, or croquet, and swimming in the pool. Also, there was more trust. At Tabor Farm Resort, doors were not locked, which surprised many of the Chicagoans. (Photo courtesy of the Bachunas Trust.)

Skits, mock weddings, and dressing in funny costumes played an important part in camaraderie between guests and staff. "Crazy golf" at Tabor Farm Resort, pictured here, was one such activity. At Birchwood Beach in Harbert, huge preparations would be made for the launch of a kerosene-fueled paper balloon as part of a skit. Eugenia Siefer remembers the mock wedding held at the Fruit Farm Resort, and Jane Granzow Miles recalls elaborate talent shows at the Manley Resort during World War II. (Photo courtesy of the Bachunas Trust.)

This is the appetizer table at Tabor Farm Resort. Ted Bachunas explains, "The entire resort centered around food with three good meals a day, including a smorgasbord appetizer buffet for the evening meal, and a open-all-the-time kitchen for the guests to raid the refrigerator and help themselves to a snack. The guests never went to bed hungry." George Chapman, who was the resort's chef from 1930 to 1958, and "Peaches," a breakfast cook at the same time, added their culinary accomplishments to the menu, including Southern meat pie and "Tabor Farm fried chicken." (Photo courtesy of Fort Miami Heritage Society.)

Hayrides have been part of Berrien County resort culture since the turn of the 20th century. At Tabor Farm Resort, in the 1930s and 1940s, two wagons were outfitted with a two-horse team. Lanterns lit the way down the local roads on evening rides. Ted Bachunas, the son of Al Bachunas, notes: "(Visitors) would have song competitions between the two wagons and would sing songs like 'Down by the Old Mill Stream,' 'You Are My Sunshine,' and 'My Gal Sal.' Any song from the First World War, I can sing it to you because of the hayrides." (Photo courtesy of Fort Miami Heritage Society.)

Not all Chicagoans who sought to escape the diseases of the city did so. This *News-Palladium* article from August 10, 1909—under the headline "State Troops May Come if Necessary to Establish Rigid Small Pox Quarantine"—reports that 100 resort guests were quarantined under armed guard at the Lord's Resort, an Oronoco Township resort which catered to Jewish guests, after township authorities discovered a child suffering from the disease. Over 100 resorters were vaccinated.

SCENE AT PENNELLWOOD, BERRIEN SPRINGS, MICH.   HENRY KEPHART & SON

Edgar S. Pennel and his wife Mary established Pennellwood in 1893, when they decided to take in boarders at the farm they purchased during the 1850s. According to present owner David Stacey, as the popularity of the resort grew, the Pennells allowed the guests to build their own cabins. The guests enjoyed swimming in the river, boating, fishing, and eating three hearty meals a day in the Red Lodge, a building constructed in 1873. Today, the smell of fresh-baked bread permeates the dining lodge, since Stacey continues to bake fresh bread from his grandmother's 90-year-old recipe. (Postcard courtesy of the Pennellwood Resort Archives.)

These guests of the 1940s or 1950s enjoy the same things that made the Pennellwood Resort a success in 1893—a peaceful retreat with good homegrown and homemade food and plenty of activities. Since there are no TVs or computers, it makes it easier for the guests to truly get away from the hurly-burly of modern life and revert to an earlier, easier time. Pennellwood has 40 log cabins as well as a six-unit motel, and continues to serve family-style meals. It is the only resort of its kind left in the state of Michigan. (Photo courtesy of the Pennellwood Resort Archives.)

Those who vacation in Michigan know the joys of fresh fruit. Cool watermelon enjoyed under a shady tree remains a delightful summer pleasure. During the heyday of resorts, families enjoyed fruits and vegetables freshly picked at the farms or bought at the Benton Harbor fruit market. John Rassogianis, whose family has a second home in Stevensville, describes helping his Uncle George can pears, peaches, blackberry jelly, grape jelly, and tomatoes. "There's just something real nice about doing the simple things like that when you're a kid." (Photo courtesy of the Pennellwood Resort Archives.)

Many of the children who happily participated in the activities of the Pennellwood Resort came back as adults with their own children. Owner David Stacey reports that there are families who have been coming to Pennellwood for more than 50 years. The resort continues to offer planned activities for children and entertainment for adults. The website says, "Don't be surprised if your waitress should challenge you to a tennis match or show up as an actress at an evening event. The staff and guests are sort of one big family." (Photo courtesy of the Pennellwood Resort Archives.)

This little boy and girl enjoy horseback riding at Pennellwood Resort. (Photo courtesy of the Pennellwood Resort Archives.)

Colonel H.E. Eastman, the distinguished gentleman with the beard on the left, established Eastman Springs Resort in Benton Township. This resort appealed to those seeking a healthful alternative to city living and was popular from the 1890s through 1920s. The spring water on the property, which was bottled and sold, attracted many for its health benefits. The resort also had mud baths. The House of David purchased 33 acres from the Eastman family in 1907 and opened their amusement park the following year. Mary's City of David purchased 54 acres in 1945. Visitors can still enjoy summer tours of the Eastman Springs property that Mary's City of David purchased in 1945, as well as see Mary's City of David Museum. Six of the original 27 springs have been cleaned and the Silver Queen supplies good drinking water. (Photo courtesy of Fort Miami Heritage Society.)

Three
SILVER BEACH AND
OTHER ATTRACTIONS

This image shows Silver Beach's Sea Swing and the Water Toboggan. (Postcard courtesy of Fort Miami Heritage Society.)

This artist's rendition of Silver Beach shows the roller coaster, a popular ride added in 1905. Silver Beach's history dates back to 1892, when Louis Wallace and Logan Drake bought land along Lake Michigan in St. Joseph. To take advantage of tourism, they built 10 cabins and later added another 70. Drake and Wallace also built several boats which cruised the St. Joseph River from the 1890s to 1924. Early photos of Silver Beach Amusement Park show a wooden boardwalk where concessionaires hawked various products and games of chance kept things lively. Three buildings were erected in the 1910s: the bathhouse and swimming pool, the roller rink, and the pavilion. The House of Mysteries also enhanced patrons' enjoyment, scaring them when they groped along the maze in the dark and surprising them with fake trap doors. In the summer of 1905, large crowds assembled to watch Johnny Morrison, a local pugilist, at the pavilion. However, the matches were suspended that year after the City of St. Joseph enacted a law against prize fighting. By 1905, billiards and bowling became available to men; women did not play such games. But both men and women enjoyed the roller coaster, shown above, and the roller rink, which had a skating floor of 60 by 138 feet. When it opened, 600 pair of skates (the kind that attached to shoes with leather straps) were available for rent. On one day in 1906, the paper reported that there were 1,500 people on the roller rink floor. This was topped by a figure later that year; when "almost 5,000 people" danced, made possible because the floor was cleared after each dance. Patrons also came for baseball games and cultural events. Of course, water sports were ever-popular; in 1906, the Evening Press reported that the beach had 30,000 patrons on a single day. Swimmers had the option of "surf-bathing" in the lake or swimming in the large natatorium, filled with steam-heated lake water. At the bathhouse, swimmers could rent suits, caps, bloomers, umbrellas, and even water wings. In the 1910s, children begged their parents to go on a ride where they sat in wagons pulled by dogs. The Airship Swing was a ride consisting of six airplanes suspended on steel cables and swinging around in a circle. The "Roaring 20s" ushered in a variety of rides and attractions as well as a new dancing hall, called Shadowland. Ted Wheems, Wayne King, Glen Miller, and Lawrence Welk played at Shadowland. The old dance hall became the Fun House, which included the Mirror Maze, Revolving Barrel, Spinning Saucer, and a huge wooden slide. Other attractions were the carousel, purchased in 1930, and rides like the Whip and Bumper Cars. In the 1930s, Louis Wallace sold Logan Drake his share of Silver Beach. Drake went on to make several additions, including the Ferris wheel, the miniature train, and Wild West shows. After Drake's death, his son-in-law operated the park for two decades, but by the 1970s, the amusement park closed, and Shadowland saw its last days in 1981. For those who spent fun-filled days and nights at the amusement park, only memories remain. Silver Beach is now a county park where swimmers still enjoy the lakefront.

Pictured here are the bathhouse, beach, and slides at Silver Beach Amusement Park. (Postcard courtesy of Fort Miami Heritage Society.)

This is an 1898 photo of the side-paddle steamer, the *Tourist*, one of Drake and Wallace's riverboats. Other boats they built included the sleek *Wolverine*, which was named after Michigan's state animal, the *Buckeye*, and the *Milton D.*, a gasoline-powered boat that they launched in 1915. They named the *Milton D.* after Drake's son. The boats seated 50 to 100 people and cruised the St. Joseph River from the 1890s to 1924. The river boats traveled from St. Joseph to Berrien Springs. (Photo courtesy of Fort Miami Heritage Society.)

Swimmers enjoy the Silver Beach Natatorium, *c.* 1910. Note the reflection in the large pool of the gallery and the windows. The pool, with water heated by steam, was "state of the art" at the time. (Postcard courtesy of Joyce Collier.)

In the background is the "Aeroplane in Action." The airplane ride was made of six airplanes of pre-World War I design suspended on steel cables and swinging around in a circle.

This postcard, postmarked August 24, 1926, bears the message: "August afternoon on Silver Beach in St. Joseph. SS *Benton Harbor* outward." Contrary to what is pictured in this postcard, the vacationer who sent this card experienced rain instead of sun. He wrote, "Crossed the lake in a steamer like you see in this picture. It rains here almost every day." Rain did not bother Mike Economos, whose family had a home in Stevensville in the 1950s and 1960s. In an interview conducted through the Berrien County Historical Association and Columbia College Chicago, he recalled: "One of my favorite things was when we would go to the beach and then a storm would be coming across the lake. We would sit up in the dunes and watch the storm come over with the lightning and everything on the clouds and the thunder and everything. And we would race until it got right close to us, then we would run home to see if we could beat the rain home." (Postcard courtesy of Fort Miami Heritage Society.)

This Silver Beach brochure shows the carousel as well as other attractions. According to a bill of sale in Daryl Schlender's collection, the carousel was purchased on November 12, 1930. The sellers were Elizabeth Dolle and M.D. Borelli. The three-row Coney Island-style machine manufactured by Fred Dolle included 41 magnificent hand-carved horses designed by Charles Carmel and three designed by Marcus Charles Illions. Music came from a beautiful eight-by-eight-foot hand-carved organ stationed in the center of the ride. Two Wurlitzer organs replaced it. When the Silver Beach Amusement Park closed in 1971, a collector bought the carousel. In 2004, in remembrance of the carousel, artists decorated 53 horses which colorfully adorned the streets of St. Joseph. The Silver Beach Carousel Society hopes to install a carousel ride once again at Silver Beach. (Brochure courtesy of Silver Beach Archives.)

Shadowland Ballroom was added to Silver Beach in 1927. In the 1930s, marathon dances were held, offering cash prizes. The ballroom became a favorite meeting place for young men and women. (Postcard courtesy of Fort Miami Heritage Society.)

This photo captures the marathon dances which took place at the Crystal Palace in the 1930s. The back of the card has the 1930 schedule: July 18 to Sept. 17. Bleacher seats for spectators cost 50¢. The couple that danced the longest got a cash prize, and at one of the dances the one voted most popular won a car—quite a deal during Depression years! (Photo courtesy of Dick Grau.)

Note the tired Shadowland marathon dancers who participated in an exhausting exhibit of stamina in order to win cash prizes. The dances were held for 24-hour periods during the Depression, in the 1930s. The girl on the left rests her head on her partner's shoulder. The young man in the right foreground is bent down in exhaustion. It is reported that the dancers were given 15-minute breaks every hour. (Postcard courtesy of Dick Grau.)

The original Silver Beach roller coaster had a view of the lighthouse and was called Figure Eight or Chase through the Clouds. Individual cars sat four people. On the top is the more modern roller coaster called the Velvet Coaster or Comet. (Photos courtesy of Silver Beach Archives.)

This view of Silver Beach shows the amusement park as it appeared in the late 1950s or early 1960s. Note Shadowland Pavilion and the merry-go-round in the right front. Of course the roller coaster is easy to spot. Silver Beach Amusement and Realty closed in August of 1970. Wreckers burned what remained in 1975. In the late 1980s, the Berrien County Parks Department purchased the site, and it now serves as a park. (Photo courtesy of Fort Miami Heritage Society.)

This is a photo of Miller's Fruit Farm stand in Stevensville near Glenlord Road. Fresh fruit can still be obtained at stands such as these, sometimes at the side of country roads where farmers leave their produce with just a can where you deposit the money. There are also farmers' markets in Bridgman, St. Joseph, or Benton Harbor, and stands such as Jackson's in New Buffalo or Fruit Acres in Coloma. Produce can be freshly picked by the buyer, at U-Pick family farms such as Stover's in Berrien Springs, which offers a variety of fruits and vegetables, or Tree-Mendus Fruit in Eau Claire. Every Fourth of July, Tree-Mendus Fruit of Eau Claire, a 520-acre farm, holds its annual Cherry Pit Spitting Contest. Herb Teichman boasts that the farm contained 300 varieties of apples from around the world, including 50 older apple varieties. Many of the U-Pick farms in Berrien County were established after the farmers had a difficult time making a profit selling wholesale. A directory published by the Michigan Department of Agriculture lists 23 U-Pick and farmers' markets in Berrien County, and there may be even more. Fresh fruit has always been a summertime delight for visitors to Berrien County, as noted in interviews conducted through the Berrien County Historical Association and Columbia College Chicago. In one such interview, Bill Rantis described his love affair with peaches while he was visiting his uncle Nick Rantis' home. "There were always peaches and I'll tell you if you've ever picked a peach off a tree and eaten it, I mean it doesn't get any better, at least for me," said Rantis. Another interviewee, Didi Tatootles, said, "We liked to go to the farm and pick fruits, and everything tasted so much better there. The tomatoes were actually tomatoes instead of the stuff we eat now. And I can remember my mother making fresh raspberry pie, raspberry being my favorite fruit. We'd go to the farm, pick raspberries, and she'd make pie. And cherry pie." (Photo courtesy of Fort Miami Heritage Society.)

Miss Sodus is pictured in this Blossomtime Parade photo. Fred L. Granger and Reverend Joshua O. Randall's idea of a floral parade to celebrate the blossoming of fruit trees fell on fruitful soil when they approached the St. Joseph Chamber of Commerce, the Rotary Club, and the Exchange Club. With the assistance of these organizations, the first Blossomtime Parade was held in May of 1923. They promoted the parade by driving a decorated truck around Chicago's Loop. The parade was discontinued in 1943 because of World War II, but started up again in 1952, and continues today with the participation of more than 20 surrounding communities and numerous organizations. Each year, on a Saturday afternoon in May, marching bands and beautiful floats wind their way from St. Joseph to Benton Harbor. The festivities now draw about 250,000 spectators. (Photo courtesy of Fort Miami Heritage Society.)

The message written on this 1927 photo reads, "In front of Benton Harbor high school on Colfax. At least 30 little floats led by the little." (Photo courtesy of Fort Miami Heritage Society.)

These three beauties participated in the 2004 Blossomtime Parade, riding in the Four Flags Area Apple Festival float. Pictured from left to right are Senior Queen Irma Reed, Princess Haileigh Trujillo, and Junior Miss Angel Brown. The festival started in 1972 when a committee of community-spirited volunteers gathered in Niles, Michigan, with the mission to promote, unite, and cherish the apple harvest through an annual festival. The week-long festival takes place at the festival grounds in Niles. Many parades and festivals add to the excitement that brings tourists to Berrien County. They include Three Oaks' Flag Day Parade, Coloma's Glad-Peach Festival, as well as the many parades celebrating holidays such as Memorial Day, the Fourth of July, and Labor Day. (Photo by Elaine Thomopoulos.)

Bands entertained both vacationers and the locals, whether it was at a parade or at a dance hall. This is the Three Oaks Military Band. An original band uniform is displayed at the Three Oaks Township Public Library. (Photo courtesy of the Three Oaks Township Public Library.)

The St. Joseph Municipal Band performs in 1986. Throughout the years music and theatre have been an attraction to Berrien County visitors. (Photo courtesy of Fort Miami Heritage Society.)

Cecil Potts founded Deer Forest in 1949, amongst an oak forest in Coloma. Children took delight in the animals and Disney-like animated displays in the park. Other attractions included a train ride and stage and animal shows. As many as 8,000 visitors a day came in the 1950s and early 1960s. People who visited Deer Forest during that era now bring their grandchildren, who enjoy the petting zoo and its 40 species of animals. Deer Forest also features Storybook Lane, a Ferris wheel, and a 4,200-square-foot "Wild Child" Play structure. The park has had several owners. The Hilton family bought it in 1993 and continues to operate it, bringing happiness to thousands of children.

The Berrien County Youth Fair started in 1946 at the Indian Field, or the Grove, with the Berrien County Agricultural Association as an official sponsor. There were 350 exhibits. In 1948, they changed their name to the Berrien County Youth Fair. The County Board of Supervisors bought 34 acres for a permanent fairground and gave the association a 99-year lease for one dollar. More land has been purchased since that time and many buildings have been built, many of them through volunteers' efforts. (Photo courtesy of Fort Miami Heritage Society.)

Chuck Nelson, the director of Sarett Nature Center in Benton Township, gets the attention of a group of youngsters in this photo. Sarett Nature Center offers guided tours and lectures about plants and animals as well as cross-country skiing in winter. Its original 130 acres (now nearly 1,000) were donated by Elizabeth Upton Vawter and William Vawter II. In 1964, the center was dedicated in the memory of Lew Sarett (Saretsky), a Northwestern University professor and Pulitzer Prize-winner who wrote about nature and the American Indian, and also a friend of William Vawter. Another nature center is Fernwood, in Niles, which opened to the public in 1964. The former home and gardens of Kay and Walter Boydston now serve as a 105-acre educational center that includes trails, tall-grass prairie, botanical gardens, a green house, science classroom, lilac and shade gardens, an arboreturn, gift shop, and café. Love Creek Nature Center, located on 110 acres in Berrien Springs, offers educational programs as well as groomed trails for cross-country skiing. (Photo courtesy of Sarett Nature Center.)

This photo of a boy and two raccoons was taken several years ago at Sarett Nature Center. One of the appeals of Berrien County is its abundant wildlife. Mammals found here include beaver, raccoon, coyote, woodchuck, otter, opossum, skunk, mice, rat, weasel, fox, bat, shrew, lemming, vole, mole, rabbit, deer, and squirrel. (Photo courtesy of Sarett Nature Center.)

Outdoor theatres were popular attractions in the 1950s and 1960s. This postcard shows the Niles Outdoor Theatre located on U.S. 31, south of Niles, Michigan. Janice Georgandas describes the Stevensville Outdoor Theater, where the movies were projected on a huge screen and the audience sat in their cars to view the latest attractions. "We used to go fourteen of us in a car together, because we paid by the car. And they luckily had seats outside so we could sit, but usually you got mosquito bitten to death." Al Coulolias remembers, "We used to put kids in the trunk and try to get them in—just like you see in the movies, and we'd get away with it." (Postcard courtesy Robert Rosenbaum.)

To celebrate the area's maritime heritage, several boat owners organized the first Venetian Festival in 1979. It started with a picnic on the river's edge and a small boat parade. It has since grown into the premier event in Michigan's Great Southwest, attracting nearly 150,000 during its four-day run. The festival now features two entertainment stages, volleyball tournaments, 5K and 10K runs, a craft show, a carnival, wine tasting, a classic car show, 45 food booths, fireworks, an outdoor big band dance, and many other events. (Photo courtesy of Fort Miami Heritage Society.)

The 25,000-year-old Bear Cave, the only one of its kind in the Great Lakes area, amazes visitors with colored stalactites, flowstone, and petrified leaves and vegetation. It is located four miles north of Buchanan along the Red Bud Trail. The cave, formed in rare "tufa rock" (a secondary limestone), rests on a glacial drift deposited during the last ice age. According to legend, in 1875, bank robbers stashed their goods there. It was this event that led to the cave's inclusion in the 1903 movie "The Great Train Robbery." There is evidence that the Potawatami Indians used the cave and also that it was used in the Underground Railroad to hide escaping slaves. The Bear Cave complex has chalets, campsites, and tent sites, along with a swimming pool, hot tub and sauna. (Postcard courtesy of Floyd and Donna Jerdon.)

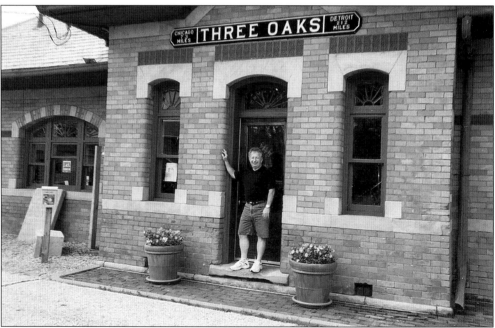

Bryan Volstrof stands in front of the Three Oaks Bicycle Museum, which used to be the Three Oaks Railroad Station. Annually Three Oaks hosts the Apple Cider Century, a bicycle tour. During the first tour, in 1974, 226 cyclists braved rain and cold winds. In the 1990s, attendance grew to 7,000. However, in 2004 the number of riders had dropped to under 5,000, because biking had lost some of its popularity amongst younger riders. In 2003, more cyclists between the ages of 70 and 79 registered than between 16 and 30. During a Sunday in late September, participants choose to bike 25, 50, 75, or 100 miles for enjoyment only—it is not a race or an endurance test, and people of all ages are welcome to participate. (Photo by Elaine Thomopoulos.)

This photo from the early or mid-1960s shows the St. Joseph Art Fair in its early days. Some of the artists at the first art fair in 1961 hung their work from clotheslines. Now the art fair is more sophisticated, with more than 200 artists participating. Every July, the juried art show attracts approximately 70,000 visitors. Benton Harbor hosts a Children's Art Fair (on the same weekend as the St. Joseph Art Fair) and the Fall Festival of the Arts in autumn. Krasl Art Center in St. Joseph offers changing art exhibits year-round as well as classes and trips. St. Joseph's other cultural attractions include the Box Factory, Curious Kid's Museum, and the Fort Miami Historical Society. (Photo courtesy of Krasl Art Center and the Krasl Art Fair on the Bluff.)

The downtowns of both St. Joseph and Benton Harbor continue to attract visitors today with retail shops, dining, and art. Here is a group outside of Kilwin's, a favorite ice cream and candy shop in St. Joseph. From left to right are Janet Dykstra, Congressman Fred Upton and Louie Rudloff, accordion player. Benton Harbor, just across the river from St. Joseph, is noted for its Arts District, which includes the Richard Hunt Studio. The studio displays the world-renowned artist's sculptures, as well the work of other artists, including the photos of innovative holographer Jesus Lopez, the studio's director. In addition, Richard Hunt displays his unique collection of African art. (Photo courtesy of Kilwin's.)

Not all visitors to Berrien County were families on vacation. Gangsters also made Berrien County their hangout and hideout. Al Capone often came to Berrien County. Countless homes, hotels, and resorts throughout Berrien County boast, "Capone stayed here." The submachine gun pictured here belonged to Fred Burke, one of Capone's associates and a supposed hit man. Police found the gun in Burke's rented Stevensville home after Burke shot and killed a St. Joseph policeman, Charles Skelley, in 1929. The sheriff's department displayed the gun, made famous because of its use in the St. Valentine's Day Massacre in Chicago, at the 2004 Berrien County Historical Association's Annual Meeting. Pictured here are Undersheriff Chuck Heit (at left) with Lieutenant Michael Kline (holding the gun). (Photo by Elaine Thomopoulos.)

According to information from Katheryn S. Zerler's *Talk of the Towns*, this is "Popcorn Jenny" (center, wearing white) with her staff in the 1890s. The person in the front left is supposedly the bouncer. Popcorn Jenny and her crew serviced sailors and steamboat passengers, as well as local men, at her place of business near the docks in downtown St. Joseph. (Photo courtesy of Dick Grau.)

From 1896 to 1926, St. Joseph attracted many loving couples who came to the city to be married since there was no wait for a license. According to a 1946 *News-Palladium* story, John F. Needham, who served as Berrien County clerk from 1896 to 1899, sold the plan of issuing licenses without a wait to Andrew Crawford, a major stockholder in Graham & Morton Boat line. Crawford printed and distributed advertising pamphlets in Chicago suggesting St. Joseph as an ideal spot for marriage and a honeymoon. According to the newspaper article, "Those were the times when a constable stationed himself at the Hotel Whitcomb bluff, at the top of the incline up from the boat docks, and there conveniently spotted likely intended brides and grooms. He wore a conspicuous badge and when the prospect approached him he lined them into columns and marched them off to the county clerk and subsequently to marrying justices and parsons. In those days the general procedure was for a couple to leave Chicago on a late morning boat, arrive in St. Joseph about 2:30, be married and return to Chicago by evening. It was common for parsons and justices of the peace to perform a couple dozen marriages on a weekend afternoon. Then arm in arm or hand in hand the newlyweds strolled up and down through Lake Bluff Park, waiting of the boat back home. The marriage business boomed, with work not only for the minister and justices of the peace, but also for hotels, restaurants, jewelers, clothiers and livery stable operators." When a law requiring a wait of five days went into effect, the number of licenses issued fell from 1,447 in 1925 to 650 in 1926. (Photo courtesy of Fort Miami Heritage Society.)

The Auscos, the semi-professional team from Benton Harbor's Ausco Products Inc., played a historic game against the Chicago White Sox at St. Joseph's Edgewater Baseball Park on July 15, 1957, attracting record crowds. From left to right are umpires Hank D'Agostino and Eldon Stover, Chicago manager Al Lopez, Ausco Manager Carl Fiore, and umpires Bill Laukus and Fred Radde. (Photo courtesy of Fort Miami Heritage Society.)

These women pose with the Dewey Cannon in Dewey Cannon Park in Three Oaks. The slogan of Three Oaks was, "Three Oaks Against the World," a result of their competition to beat the rest of the nation in contributing the largest amount per capita to a fund for a national memorial to the soldiers and sailors who lost their lives in the Spanish-American War. Three Oaks beat the other towns and received this ancient cannon which had been taken by Admiral Dewey during the Spanish-American War. Thousands came to see President McKinley when he came to Three Oaks for the presentation of the cannon on October 17, 1899. (Photo courtesy of the Three Oaks Township Public Library.)

Four

CAMPS

These young women enjoy the water at Forest Beach Camp in New Buffalo Township. According to the *New Buffalo Story*, Dr. Barlow first developed the property with the intention of its becoming a health sanitarium, but he died before its completion. His son then operated the facilities as a resort until 1916. When the YWCA took over, it was named as Camp YO-WO-CHA. Girls who attended the camp enjoyed swimming, nature study, athletics, picnics, hiking, and beach parties. The YWCA sold the property in 1988. There were several camps for Jewish children in Berrien County. They included Tel Chai in New Buffalo, Camp Hadais on Lake Shore Drive south of Gordon Beach, Camps Avodah and Sharon on Clear Lake in Buchanan, and on Paw Paw Lake, Camp Zahavo for Girls and Camp Achim for Boys. Berrien County also became home to several scout camps. They included Camp Madron in Buchanan, a 360-acre Boy Scout camp which later became a second-home community, and Camps Betz and Soni Springs which continue to welcome scouts. Frank Betz, a Hammond surgical manufacturer and philanthropist, bought land in Berrien Springs on which the Boy Scouts from the Hammond area established Camp Betz. On June 9, 1924, Camp Frank J. Betz officially opened for three two-week periods. Soni Springs, a camp established by the Northern Indiana Girl Scout Council, began financing a "camp fund" in 1959. They set aside 16¢ per box of cookie profit for the camp, and had such success that they purchased land in Three Oaks that same year. The camp, complete with a lake, was dedicated as Camp Soni Springs in 1963. The name is an acronym for the Scouts of Northern Indiana (SONI). (Postcard courtesy of Robert Rosenbaum.)

These are the Bluebird and Big Bear buildings at Forest Beach Camp. (Postcard courtesy of Robert Rosenbaum.)

This image shows the interior of Hoover Hall at the YWCA's Forest Beach Camp in New Buffalo Township. (Postcard courtesy of Robert Rosenbaum.)

This card shows a beautiful silhouette against the sunset. It is reported to be an image of the YMCA Forest Beach Camp in New Buffalo. Girls who attended the camp enjoyed swimming, nature study, athletics, picnics, hiking, and beach parties. (Postcard courtesy of Robert Rosenbaum.)

SILHOUETTE, Y. W. C. A. FOREST BEACH CAMP, NEW BUFFALO, MICH.   ID-NBMR

Twilight Camp-Fire Service on the Beach, Tower Hill Camp, Sawyer, Mich.   39923-9

Tower Hill Camp ended a perfect day with this twilight campfire service on the beach. In 1922, E.K. Warren bequeathed a house and 193 feet of lake frontage in Sawyer to the Congregational Conference of Illinois. The camp's opening ceremonies were held on June 21, 1924. The church also owned a beach house, which Chicago visitors took advantage of to rent bathing suits, caps, and towels. The beach house is said to have been a bordello used by the sailors and lumberjacks of the Sawyer area after the Chicago fire. The camp is now operated under the auspices of the United Church of Christ, which came into being in 1957 when the Evangelical and Reformed Church and the Congregational Christian Churches united. (Postcard courtesy of Floyd and Donna Jerdon.)

Swimming was a favorite activity for children attending the Chicago Commons Farm Camp. (Postcard courtesy of Robert Rosenbaum.)

Girls slept in these cabins at the Chicago Commons Farm Camp on Maudlin Road in New Buffalo. The Chicago Commons operated this camp for girls and boys from Chicago between the 1920s and the 1980s. City children attended the camp free or for a nominal fee. The camp offered an opportunity for city kids from Chicago to enjoy the country life. (Postcard courtesy of Robert Rosenbaum.)

Camp Marie Du Lac, directed by the Sisters of the Holy Cross of Holy Cross, Indiana, opened in June of 1943. The Lakeside camp served girls aged five through 17. According to the book *Facts and Fancies of Lakeside*, published in 1945, activities included attendance at Holy Mass (optional), instruction in arts and crafts, swimming, horseback riding, and sports such as tennis, softball, volleyball, and badminton, as well as dancing and dramatics in the recreation pavilion. Other activities included ping-pong, shuffleboard, deck tennis, and darts. (Postcard courtesy of Robert Rosenbaum.)

This postcard of the Aquatic Camp bears the postmark "Benton Harbor, 1909." The message reads, "Dear, Sister, Send this to show what kind of a time I having. They are across the river these lady [*sic*] are visiting here for the day. I remain as ever you brother John." In the margin he writes, "Tell Frances I not coming home no more." (Postcard courtesy of Benton Harbor Public Library.)

This is a view of Lake Chapin and Camp Oronoko's Stone Bungalow in Berrien Springs, The camp's slogan was "A Camp for All Ages and Creeds." An article written by Rev. John Crippen Evans for the July 28, 1929 issue of the *Tribune* described the boys from the Chicago Heart Society who came to the camp, "There they go! Sixty of them! Splash! Sixty splashes merge into one. The waters of the sleepy St. Joe River become greatly troubled, but sixty boys from Camp Oronoko are not." In a letter to Camp Director Frederick C. Spalding, Mrs. Gertrude Howe Britton, the head of the Heart Society, related the gratitude the boys were unable to express for themselves, "Until you did give us this opportunity at Camp Oronoko," Mrs. Britton's letter stated, "there was no place we could send boys 14 years of age and over." The camp closed in 1941, after they discovered that the children could no longer swim in the St. Joseph River because of pollution. Other children's camps in this part of Berrien County were Camp Avodah and Camp Sharon, camps for Jewish children on Clear Lake in Buchanan. They were both established by the Chicago Board of Jewish Education in 1946. Camp Sharon was for boys and girls and emphasized the study of Hebrew language and literature, while Camp Avodah was an eight-week work camp for boys aged 12 to 17. According to Walter Roth, the current president of the Chicago Jewish Historical Society who attended the camp in 1946, the boys worked on local farms, weeding, hoeing, and picking fruits and vegetables in the morning. In the afternoon they cleaned up, rested, swam, and played sports. The boys also helped put up the khaki-colored permanent barracks and participated in cultural programs. During the first year of the camp, there were about 100 boys, including about 25 boys from the Marks Nathan Home, a Jewish orphanage. A brochure explains the mission of the camp: "Avodah is a self-governing community where the emphasis is on a well balanced program of physical, social, agricultural, and Jewish cultural activities, with particular attention given to individual needs. The spirit and inspiration of Judaism and Americanism are embodied in its daily life. Out of this environment emerge the Jewish leaders of tomorrow." A Christian church bought Camp Avodah in the 1960s. (Postcard courtesy of Floyd and Donna Jerdon.)

LADIES' QUARTER – ŽENSKÁ ČTVŘÍ

"Ladies Quarters" is printed on this postcard in English and Czech. Lillian Prince Abrahamson, in an article about Camp Sokol in Union Pier, recalled the early days, "I Remember! The summer days spent at the 'Old Camp' when I was in my early teens; sleeping in tents (which would be a hardship now, but fun then); forming lasting friendships with my 'Tent Mates;' the delicious meals prepared by Faninka who came to cook summer after summer; the antics of the 'Dirty Dozen,' a group of young men sometimes boisterous but funny and witty and always gentlemen; the Saturday night dances in town and the beach parties afterward—all wonderful memories." Gymnastics, song, and dance were also part of the camp experience. (Postcard courtesy of Robert Rosenbaum.)

In this photo by Boundnek, Czech-American gymnasts show their muscles at Sokol Camp in New Buffalo, Michigan, c. 1925. Sokol continues its programs for children, youth, and families today. The camp was established in 1904 by the Plzensky Sokol located in the Pilsen neighborhood of Chicago. Sokol is a Czecholovakian gymnastic, cultural, and educational organization. The first campers slept in tents at a site one-half mile from present-day New Buffalo. Today the camp is located on property adjacent to Lake Michigan which was purchased in 1924. (Photo courtesy of American Sokol Organization.)

The New First Church Camp of the First Congregational Church of Chicago was located in Bridgman, just south of Weko Beach on the lakefront. Bob Beaver writes that his grandparents, James and Effie Null, served as caregivers there in the 1960s and that they would rent it to churches from Chicago and Northeastern Indiana. The whole area was called "Marwood Dunes" and they offered beach activities as well as basketball (there's a full-size court buried under 15 feet of sand next to the old stairs). Beaver recalls, "I can still hear the waves from the lake as it sounded from my grandparents' cabin and the lodge. That will always be with me." The camp was sold to the State of Michigan and added to the acreage of Warren Dunes State Park. (Postcard courtesy of Robert Rosenbaum.)

Faculty and students are pictured at the Leadership Training School at Camp Warren, c. 1921. The former Berrien County Sunday School Association founded Camp Warren as a Sunday school camp. The old Higman Park golf grounds and clubhouse served as the site of the first church camp in 1913. Soon the camp moved to the former Pottawatomie Park, donated by J.N. Klock, with the stipulation that the camp be named after E.K. Warren of Three Oaks. The camp included 20 acres on the shore of Lake Michigan, located off M-63, north of Benton Harbor. A 1921 booklet entitled the *Berrien Booster* reads: "Those who attended the course will go back to their home equipped to extend the scope and usefulness of their Sunday Schools in a manner to benefit the entire community." The camp was sold in the 1990s. (Image from booklet *Berrien Booster* courtesy of the Benton Harbor Public Library.)

The German District of the Assemblies of God Church purchased 80 acres off Church Street in Bridgman to build a camp serving parishioners, which they named Bethel Park. Beginning in the late 1940s, they conducted a family camp for 10 to 14 days. Families continue to come from across the United States. At the camp, church services are conducted in both English and German. Reverend David D. Rueb reports that the English services have better attendance. To meet the expense of maintaining the camp, Bethel Park also hosts Christian groups, sports camps, retreats, parties, and business meetings. (Photo courtesy of German District of the Assemblies of God Church.)

This photo of vacationers camping out, *c.* 1906, may have been taken at Camp Sheffield at Sister's Lake, which is located just outside of Berrien County. It captures the camping craze popular at that time. Campers wanted to get back to nature and healthful living. Also, it was less expensive than going to the resorts. (Photo courtesy of Fort Miami Heritage Society.)

These young men enjoy themselves by camping on the river in the 1890s. The sign on the boat says, "You and I and All of Us by the Sea." The notation on the photo says that "Hatch and friends" are pictured. (Photo courtesy of Fort Miami Heritage Society.)

Five

HOUSE OF DAVID

While the House of David's amusement park was known throughout the nation, as were its baseball teams and jazz bands, the community's religious tenets were not as well known. In 1903, Benjamin and Mary Purnell (pictured second from right and fourth from right) came to Benton Harbor with five followers, and by 1919, the communal society they founded had grown to include 1,000 members, including Edith Meldrim (left), Cora Mooney (second from left), and Ada Ross (third from right). The Israelite House of David believe that upon the second coming of Christ, 144,000 worthy couples gathered from the 12 tribes of Israel will be received body and soul into a "heaven on Earth." They believe that children born to these couples will lead the world into a perpetual state of harmony and connection to God. They also believe that God sent his teaching through seven messengers. They believe that Joanna Southcott of England was the first, and other messengers arrived following her death in 1814. In preparation for the second coming of Christ (which they believe will occur upon a millenium), they abstain from selfishness, lust, alcohol, and meat, and practice celibacy. Some followers and their families came to the House of David in Benton Harbor from as far away as Australia.

The House of David, a communal society, became self-sufficient, with members producing their own food, making their own clothing, and designing and constructing new buildings as the community grew. It became an important economic force in the greater community, as the amusement park, baseball, music, and other attractions were pivotal in attracting tourists to Southwestern Michigan. Not only did its park and attractions draw thousands of tourists per year, but the House of David also had extensive farmland and offered various goods and services to others.

In the 1920s, however, the State of Michigan waged court battles against the House of David. Difficulties also followed the death of Benjamin Purnell in 1927. The House of David then split into two factions; one was made up of followers of Mary Purnell, and the other was comprised of followers of H.T. Dewhirst, a former California judge who had joined the colony in 1921. Supporters of Mary believed that both Mary and Benjamin together were the seventh messenger, while Dewhirst's supporters believed that only Benjamin held that role. In 1930, Mary established her own colony on Britain Avenue, right down the road from the original colony. To differentiate it from the other group, she named it "the Israelite House of David as Reorganized by Mary Purnell," or Mary's City of David. The original House of David split in half: 217 of the colony's members left with Mary and 218 stayed with Dewhirst. Both communities thrived well into the 1960s, but by the late 1960s, membership had declined. According to Ron Taylor of the City of David, the following things contributed to the loss of membership: "The faith was no longer publicly preached after Mary passed away in 1953. Very minimal outreach or public interacition yielded only a few new members. The inspirational leadership was also missing; Mary and Benjamin had been a great charismatic draw. By the mid-1960s, most of the original movers and shakers had passed away. Celibacy was another important part of that whole picture." (Photo on previous page courtesy of Fort Miami Heritage Society.)

This is the House of David's Ladies' Quartet. Starting at the bottom and going clockwise, they are Florence Tulk, Eunice Baushke, Mabel Blackburn, and Bertha Bell. (Photo courtesy of Fort Miami Heritage Society.)

This photo shows the House of David bowling alley, with the House of David Girls' Band posing in front. The House of David invented an automatic pinsetter for bowling c. 1910. Fifteen of these automatic bowling alleys were set up in the park. The original bowling alley was donated to the National Bowling Hall of Fame and Museum located in St. Louis, Missouri, in 1975. (Photo courtesy of Fort Miami Heritage Society.)

These buses, used at the 1933–1934 World's Fair in Chicago, took passengers directly to the House of David from the *Theodore Roosevelt* boat. (Postcard courtesy of Fort Miami Heritage Society.)

This photo was taken in 1919. Various performers and vaudeville acts came to entertain amusement park guests. Admission was free. (Postcard courtesy of Fort Miami Heritage Society.)

Frank Rosetta (left) and Reuben Jeffries (right) man the House of David booth at the World's Fair in Chicago. The booth, open during 1933 and 1934, attracted tourists from across the nation and peaked their interest in visiting the House of David Amusement Park in Benton Harbor. Frank Rosetta created a hydro-stone process and a secret glazing finish (a shiny pearl-like finish) that made the finished sculptured creations highly prized souvenirs. The pieces ranged from small figurines and ashtrays to seven-foot statues. In 1907, at age 13, Rosetta came to the House of David with his family. Rosetta put his artistic talents to work by designing the House of David's prize-winning floats for the Blossomtime Parade. (Postcard courtesy of Fort Miami Heritage Society.)

Miniature Trains at House of David Park

**EVERYTHING IN THE WAY OF
ACCOMMODATION & ENTERTAINMENT!**

MINIATURE RAILWAY
FREE BAND CONCERTS
FREE VAUDEVILLE
HOTEL
RESTAURANT
BEER GARDENS
DANCING
BOWLING
BILLIARDS
MIDGET AUTOS
AVIARY AND ZOO

FURNISHED COTTAGES AND ROOMS

SOUVENIRS OF ALL DESCRIPTIONS!

. . You can spend a very pleasant time at the
House of David enjoying the Free Concerts
and Vaudeville at the Open-Air Theatre in the
Entertainment Gardens at our Picturesque Park
Every Afternoon & Evening During Summer!

SEE THIS MOST INTERESTING PLACE

This House of David ticket shows the various types of entertainment offered at the park in the 1930s, also noting that the park offered furnished cottages and rooms. The miniature steam railroads were a popular attraction. Mary's City of David Museum reports that over 70,000 rode the railroad in 1908, a number that rose to 84,000 in 1912. (Image courtesy of Fort Miami Heritage Society.)

IDEAL OPEN-AIR BEER GARDEN and THEATRE at HOUSE OF DAVID PARK
ENJOY THE FREE CONCERTS AND VAUDEVILLE

HOUSE OF DAVID PARK, Benton Harbor, Mich. - The place for an outing or vacation!

Here is the open-air beer garden and theater of the House of David. The House of David purchased 33 acres from the Eastman family in 1907 and opened at the Park Springs of Eden on July of 1908. On opening day, 5,000 people attended. (Postcard courtesy of Fort Miami Heritage Society.)

In 1908, the House of David purchased a miniature locomotive from New York. Members had observed these at the St. Louis World's Fair in 1904 while manning a recruiting booth there. The House of David engineers figured out how to make their own. In the late 1920s and early 1930s, seven trains carried passengers to and from the park, from the Britain Avenue Depot to the north side of the park ravine. Pat Mosher, who lives in South St. Joseph, remembers, "On a quiet night you could hear the piercing wail of the little train all the way in South St. Joseph." (Postcard courtesy of Fort Miami Heritage Society.)

The midget House of David automobiles delighted children. (Photo courtesy of Fort Miami Heritage Society.)

Exotic animals, like this leopard, attracted patrons to the House of David Zoo. The zoo was established when the park first opened in 1908 and continued until 1945, when the animals were shipped to the Lincoln Park Zoo in Chicago. (Photo courtesy of Fort Miami Heritage Society.)

Pictured from left to right are Bob Dewhirst, Joe Louis (world heavyweight boxing champion from 1937 to 1949), Bob ?, and Eddie Deal, the catcher for the House of David Baseball Team. Eddie Deal was a pilot, as well as a top-notch catcher. The Cincinnati Reds wanted to recruit him, but he preferred to stay with the House of David. In 2001, when Deal was on his deathbed at age 98, he was informed that the House of David team had again started a team. He said, "I'll be there," and rolled over and died. Another photo similar to this  one was taken in the driveway of Julian Black's home. Joe Louis' manager, Julian Black, owned a home in Stevensville which Joe and his trainer, Jack Blackburn, visited for training sessions. (Photo courtesy of Fort Miami Heritage Society.)

This is the House of David Baseball Team, *c.* 1914, prior to its becoming semi-professional. By 1917, the team joined the Intercity Baseball Association of Chicago and played teams in southwest Michigan, northern Indiana, and Chicago. They eventually barnstormed throughout the country, and played several games against professional teams. They scored victories against the St. Louis Cardinals and the Philadelphia Athletics. Summer vacationers attended the home games. Chicagoan Tom Pekras remembers the excitement of seeing Satchel Paige (the first African American inducted into the Hall of Fame) play. Both the House of David and Mary's City of David had teams. The House of David team played until the 1940s, and Mary's City of David team played until the 1950s. Today the Mary's City of David team plays vintage baseball on the restored baseball diamond located on Mary's City of David grounds. They play with the old-time baseball equipment and follow the rules of the 1850s. The "gentlemen" ballists of that day played baseball for fun and exercise. They called each other "mister" and "sir" and had certain rules, such as fining ballists 25¢ for swearing, spitting, scratching, or using alcohol or tobacco. The umpire sometimes asked the ballists and spectators for help in making decisions. Watching Mary's baseball team play today is great fun; old time refreshments, such as sarsaparilla, are available. (Photo courtesy of Fort Miami Heritage Society.)

The House of David baseball team entertained its audience by staging comedy acts at games. Pictured here is donkey baseball, a gimmick used by promoter Ray Doan. The players performed while on donkeys, except for the pitcher and catcher. Even hitters, after they hit the ball, mounted a donkey to reach the bases. The baseball team also played a game called "Pepper Ball" in which they performed silly antics, passing the ball back and forth and hiding the ball in their beards. The House of David is best known for its baseball teams, but there were basketball teams, as well, one of which traveled with the Harlem Globetrotters in Europe in the 1950s. (Photo courtesy of Fort Miami Heritage Society.)

Members of this 1919 House of David girls' baseball team included some young men. Pictured are, from left to right: (seated) Marie Falkenstein, Marge Vieritz, ? Bauschke, Marietta Smith, Jewell Boone, Dave Harrison, Elijah Burland, Mildren Vaughn, Oscar Sassman, and Luther Jackson. According to Ron Taylor of Mary's City of David, the biggest problem of the team was finding another athletic team that wore skirts to play against, since there were few women baseball teams at that time. Jewel Boone, a musician and ball-player, is in the front row, fourth from the right. Boone threw a curve ball that struck out many of the male players. Another outstanding House of David player was Jackie Mitchell, who pitched in 1933 and was the starting pitcher in the victory over the St. Louis Cardinals. Babe Didrikson Zaharias also played for the House of David team, but on the men's team, not the girls' team. (Photo courtesy of Fort Miami Heritage Society.)

The House of David presented this patriotic program on July 4, 1943, during World War II. Note the "V" for victory. The House of David Band was one of the first organizations in Michigan to receive the distinguished service citation from the Music War Council. A Sept. 23, 1944, *News-Palladium* article stated that the citation was given, "In recognition of [the band's] patriotic and inspiring use of music to aid the national war effort." (Photo courtesy of Fort Miami Heritage Society.)

The House of David presentations entertained thousands each summer. In this image, stage antics are performed on the outdoor stage. (Photo courtesy of Fort Miami Heritage Society.)

Mary's City of David built this log cabin in 1933. The original five cabins were completed in 1933 and rented out by that summer. The cabins were made with logs cut from the colony's Rocky Farm and milled at their sawmill. The stones were laid and cut by Louie Manthey, while Melvin Tucker drove the truck bringing stones from the Rocky Farm. Four of these original cabins remain; one has been completely restored and is now a year-round dwelling. Eleven acres were purchased along Eastman Avenue and East Britain Avenue after the reorganization of March 14, 1930, and tourist cabins were built on the property. The resort grew to about 200 rooms, keeping a laundry, bakery, restaurant, housekeeping, and resort personnel busy seven days a week throughout the summer. By the mid-1930s, practically all of the guests were Jewish. They continued coming until the mid-1960s. Since the cottage did not furnish cooking facilities, the restaurant served all meals. Mary's Vegetarian Restaurant opened in 1932, at 1204 East Britain. The vegetarian diet worked well for the guests, since the vegetarian meals were kosher. Fresh farm products, home-canned products, and fresh baked goods from the bakery just a block away made the vegetarian restaurant popular with local residents as well. The Gate of Prayer Synagogue was built in 1937–1938, with the cooperation and financial support from the Jewish community. Rabbi Dr. H.L. Goldstein attended the dedication of the synagogue on July 4, 1938. The last of the two remaining families turned over the synagogue keys to the trustees of the City of David in 1976. (Postcard courtesy of Fort Miami Heritage Society.)

6 Miles South of St. Joseph. Mich. on U. S. 12

This postcard shows the Grande Vista Restaurant, fountain, and Westside Courts. In 1933, the House of David built the luxurious Grande Vista tourist court on Red Arrow Highway in Stevensville. It had 28 deluxe units with kitchenettes and a café and nightclub which accommodated 500 people. Hundreds of tiny twinkling lights adorned the nightclub. Guests enjoyed dancing in the evenings with House of David talent as well as famous big bands. The carefully-crafted fountain shimmered with stalactites, quartz crystals, petrified wood, and aquamarine. The first motel proved so successful that the House of David built a second Spanish-style motel opposite the first one, on the east side of Red Arrow Highway. The museum and souvenir shop located at the East Court displayed 5,000 pieces of pottery, tools, utensils, and jewelry from the Mimbranos Indians, which had been collected by Bob Dewhirst. (Postcard courtesy of Fort Miami Heritage Society.)

The House of David sold ice cream and soft drinks at their amusement park. They were known for their caramel sugar waffle ice cream cones. They made their own ice cream from the fresh dairy products supplied by their own farms. (Photo courtesy of Fort Miami Heritage Society.)

This photo taken in front of Mary's City of David Hotel in downtown Benton Harbor is likely from the 1930s. The hotel's special hematite surface glistens when the sun strikes it. The hotel's construction started in 1922, but work was suspended in 1927. After the House of David split into two factions, the hotel was awarded to Mary's City of David and completed in 1931. The two gentlemen in the photo are Manager Bill Totten (left), who worked nights, and Assistant Manager Bob Griggs, who worked days. They each worked 12-hour shifts, from five to five. Griggs managed the hotel from mid-1932 to March 1975, working for 42 years without a day off, an awesome record of job responsibility. The hotel's restaurant served vegetarian meals, carrying on a tradition that first started when meals were served to the public at the House of David amusement park in 1908. Mary's City of David served vegetarian meals at its Britain Avenue location from 1932 to 1964 and Mary's City of David Hotel in downtown Benton Harbor from 1931 to 1974, when the hotel was exchanged for property on Lake Chapin. (Photo courtesy of Fort Miami Heritage Society.)

Performances on the House of David stage attracted thousands. According to the Israelite House of David website, the week started slow, with Monday and Tuesday having small crowds. Wednesday's Amateur Night, with Chic Bell as master of ceremonies, attracted a larger crowd because adoring families came to see their children perform. On Thursday nights, the local resorts brought their guests. Friday featured polka or square dancing and Saturday and Sunday afternoons attracted large crowds with Manna Woodword of the House of David leading the band. (Postcard courtesy of Fort Miami Heritage Society.)

BIBLIOGRAPHY

Adkin, Clare. *Brother Benjamin*. Berrien Springs, MI: Andrews University Press, 1990.

And Still We Grow: The Story of the Beginning and Growth of Three Oaks, MI. Historical material collected by members of the 1947–1948 Fifth Grade, Three Oaks Public Schools, Three Oaks, MI, Compiled by Jean R. Curren.

Anderson, Eleanor. "Spinks's Spring Bluff Resort." *Fort Miami Heritage Newsletter*. Volume 10. 1.

Anderson, Jean L. *Back in Those Golden Days Gone By*. Shorewood Hills: 1988.

Aron, Cindy. *Working at Play, A History of Vacations in the United States*. New York: Oxford University Press, 1999.

Ashcroft, Mrs. Raymond, O.T. Henkle, and Paul Hoffman (Eds.) *Facts and Fancies of Lakeside*. Women's Committee of the Chikaming Country Club, August, 1945.

Ast, William F. III. "Those Grand Old Hotels." *Herald Palladium*. February 16, 1992.

Ast, William F. III. "Once-Popular Church Camp May Be Sold." *Herald Palladium*, May 24, 1997.

Atlas and Plat Book, Berrien County, Michigan. Rockford, Ill.: Thrift Press, 1929.

Atlas of Berrien County, Michigan. Philadelphia: C.O. Titus, 1873.

Atwood, Harold A. *Historic Sites of Berrien County*. Berrien County Community Foundation, Inc., 1989.

Bainbridge Township Celebrates the Bicentennial. Bainbridge Township Board, 1976.

Ballard, Ralph. *Tales of Early Niles*. 1948.

Benton Harbor. Benton Harbor Improvement Association. Benton Harbor, Michigan: 1891.

Benton Harbor: The Metropolis of the Fruit Belt. 1915.

Benton Harbor, Michigan: Educational, Commercial, Industrial, Financial. Date unknown.

The Benton Harbor Fruit Market: Present and Proposed Facilities. Washington, D.C.: Government Printing Office, 1960.

Berrien Booster. Benton Harbor, Michigan: August, 1921.

Berrien County Historical Directory. St. Joseph: Kimball Publishing Co., 1896.

Berrien Township History and Heritage: Centuries Past Ushering in the Millennium 2000. Berrien Township Board, 1999.

Booth, Walter, Janiata Cupp, and Max Medley. *Grande Mere. A Very Special Place*. Kalamazoo, Mi: Grande Mere Assoc., 1975.

Burns, Denise. "The Spirit's Still Flowing." *Fort Miami Heritage Center Newsletter*. Dec. 1996.

Burgh, Robert. *History of the Region of Three Oaks*. Three Oaks: Edward K. Warren Foundation, 1937.

Burgoyne, Leon. *A History of Berrien Springs, Michigan*. 1946.

Buryk, P.R. "The Prairie Club of Chicago and the Michiana Dunes: Recreational Community and Preservation Ethos." A Paper Submitted to the Faculty of the Department of History in Partial Fulfillment of the Requirements for a Degree with Honors. Annapolis, Maryland, December 17, 2002.

By the Waters: Benton Harbor Centennial, 1866–1968, Benton Harbor, 1966.

Carney, James T., Ed. *Berrien Bicentennial*. Stevensville, Berrien County Bicentennial Commission, Tesar Printing Company, 1976.

Cawley, Sherry. *Berrien County Postcards*. Charleston, S.C. Arcadia Publishing, 2000.

Centennial History of Lakeside. Village of Lakeside Association Inc. 1974.

Champion, Ella. *Berrien's Beginnings*. 1926.

Chauncey, A.E. *History of Berrien County*.

Cohen, Ronald D. and Steven G. McShane, (Eds.), *Moonlight in Duneland*, Bloomington, Indiana: Indiana University Press, 1998.

Coolidge, Judge Orville. *A Twentieth Century History of Berrien County, Michigan*. Chicago: Lewis Publishing Co., 1906.

"Colored Folk Have a Resort." *News-Palladium*, August 18, 1909.

Cunningham, Wilbur. *Land of Four Flags*. Grand Rapids, Michigan: William B. Eerdmans Publishing Co., 1961.

Daniels, Alenda. *Dune Country: a Guide for Hikes and Naturalists*.

Davis, Roy. *Paw Paw River Days and Nights*. Hartford: 1993.

"Decade From 1925 to 1934 is Memorable." *News-Palladium* January 1, 1935.

Dittmer, Sharon and Kate Sheridan. "Apple Cider Cyclists Brave the Elements." *Harbor Country News*, October 2, 2003.

Dowling, Rev. Edward J. "The Dustless Road to Happyland." *Michigan History Magazine*, 1947.

"Drake and Wallace Ready to Open Their New Rink This Week." *The Evening Press*. 1905.

Eau Claire Area's Annual Cherry Festival, July 4th, Commemorating the 150th Anniversary of the State of Michigan, 1837–1987 and the 125th Anniversary of Eau Claire 1861–1986. Cherry Festival Committee, 1987.

Durkin, Eileen. "Lecture on the Irish of Grand Beach." Presented at the Irish American Heritage Center, Chicago, Illinois, April, 2003.

Echoes of Summer Time Pleasures: St. Joseph and Benton Harbor, The Twin Cities of the East Shore and Their Multitude of Attractions, St. Joseph, Michigan: Graham and Morton Transportation Company, 1893.

Ekert, Kathryn Bishop. *Buildings of Michigan*, New York: Oxford University Press, 1993.

The Farm Journal Illustrated Rural Directory of Berrien County, Michigan 1917–1922. Washington Square, Philadephia: Wilmer Atkinson Company, 1922.

Fogarty, Robert. *The Righteous Remnant*. Kent, Ohio: Kent State University Press, 1981.

Gitersonke, Don. *Baseball's Bearded Boys*. Las Vegas: 1996.

Glimpses of the Past, Published by the North Berrien Historical Society. Watervliet, Michigan: Printed by Tri-City Record, 1992.

Goetz, Betty, (Ed.) *Stevensville & Area 1884–1984*. Stevensville Village Council, Stevensville, MI: 1984.

Goodsell, Leo. "Vegetarian Foodways of the House of David and Mary's City of David." *The Other Side of the Lake*. June 2000.

Gowdy, Mrs. H.W. "Later History of Union Pier: The Summer Resort Era." *Union Pier Wave*, [1934?].

Grande Mere. Stevensville, MI: Grand Mere Association, 1973.

Graves, W.W. *Atlas of Berrien County, Michigan*. Chicago: Rand McNally & Co., 1887.

Hawkins, Joel and Terry Bertolino. *House of David Baseball Club*. Charleston, S.C.: Arcadia Publishing , 2000.

Headlight Flashes: Benton Harbor and St. Joseph, Michigan. 1898.

"Help Bring the Horses Back to the Beach!" Flier produced by the Silver Beach Carousel Society, Inc.

Herkerkner, Mrs. Robert, "Humor Highlighted in History of Twin Cities," *The Herald-Palladium*. Dec. 30, 1976.

Hesse, Marie, "Grand Beach—Has History Too—Told in Story of Grand Beach." *Grand Beach Breeze*, July 1, l938.

History of Berrien and Van Buren Counties, Michigan. Philadelphia: D.W. Ensign Co., 1880.

History of Coloma, Michigan and Program of the Centennial Celebration and Homecoming, August 20th to 23rd, 1936. Coloma Civic Association, 1936.

History of the Port of St. Joseph-Benton Harbor. 1965

Hoekstra, Dave. "Pennellwood Creates a Lifetime of Summer Memories." *Chicago Sun-Times*, Sunday, August 3, 2003.

"Hogue Raids Rokoz Hotel, Gets Liquor." *News-Palladium*, August 3, 1918.

Holtzman, Robert. "Fabulous Fruits of Freedom: A Historical Pageant Commemorating the 200th Year of America and Berrien County." Fostoria, OH, 1976.

Hunt, Don and Mary, *Hunt's Guide to West Michigan*, 1993.

I Know My Community: St. Joseph and Benton Harbor Community Study. 1944.

Images of the Past, South Haven, Michigan: 1984.

"The Indiana Dunes—Legacy of Sand, Special Report 8." State of Indiana Department of Natural Resources Geological Survey, Bloomington, Indiana, 1974.

Ivey, Paul Wesley. *The Pere Marquette Railroad Company*. The Black Letter Press, 1970.

Jensen, Jennie and Sidney Hoover. *Grand Beach*. Unpublished document of photos and ephemera.

Kelly, William. "Grand Beach History." Unpublished paper.

Kissman, Nadra. *The New Buffalo Story 1834–1976*. The New Buffalo Area Bicentennial Committee, 1976.

"Lakeside. . . At the Edge of a Great Expanse." *The Red Arrow Review*. Summer 1994.

"Lakeside Resort Burns to Ground." *News-Palladium*, October 21, 1912.

Lachler, Marge and Jean Stuebing. *Memoirs of Bethany Beach*. Cambridge, Minnesota: Sunshine Graphics, 1997.

Lawrence, Lisa. "Camp Soni Springs—a Hidden Treasure in Three Oaks," *South County Gazette*, August 25 2003.

McKelvy,Charles. "Rediscovering the Magic," *The Other Side of the Lake*, July, 2004.

Maloney, Cathy Jean Maloney. *The Prairie Club of Chicago*. Charleston, South Carolina:Arcadia Publishing, 2001.

"Mecca for Large Crowds." *News-Palladium*, August 23, 1909.

Michigan Department of Agriculture. *U-Pick Directory*. Michigan Department of Agriculture, 2003.

Morton, J.S., *Reminiscences of the Lower St. Joseph River Valley*. Benton Harbor: Federation of Women's Clubs, [1935?]

Mueller, Robert and RoseAnna. *Harbor Country*. Charleston, S.C.: Arcadia Publishing, 2003.

Myers, Robert. *Historical Sketches of Berrien County*. Berrien Springs: Berrien County Historical Association, 1988.

Myers, Robert. *Historical Sketches of Berrien County, volume 2*. Berrien Springs: Berrien County Historical Association, 1989.

Myers, Robert. *Historical Sketches of Berrien County, volume 3*. Berrien Springs: Berrien County Historical Association, 1994.

"The May Graham." *Showcase Southwestern Michigan*. Jan/Feb, 1991.

"No More Fights at Silver Beach." *The Evening Post*. 1905.

"Obituary of Irwin Rew." *Evanston Review*. February 6, 1958.

"Orphans Stir Jew and Gentile." *News-Palladium*, Aug. 18, 1909.

"Outings—Midsummer Voyages of the Fruit Region."

Pender, James. *History of Benton Harbor and Tales of Village Days*. Chicago: Braun Printing Co., 1915.

"Planks Tavern No More." *Daily Palladium*, July, 1898.

Polk's City Directory of Benton Harbor-St. Joseph. Starting from 1892.

Portrait and Biographical Record of Berrien and Cass Counties, Michigan. Biographical Publishing Co., 1893.

Preston, A.G. Jr. *Old Benton Harbor and Environs in Pictures*. 1993.

Preston, A.G. Jr. *Old St. Joseph in Pictures*, 1991.

Preston, A.G. Jr. *Drake and Wallace or the Story of Silver Beach*. 1992.

"Program, The Twin City Orchestra, Silver Beach, Sunday, August 9th, 1908." *The Evening Post*, 1908.

Rasmussen, Roderick L. *A History of Little Paw Paw Lake and Deer Forest, Michigan*. Coloma, Michigan: Southwestern Michigan Publications, 1999.

Rasmussen, Roderick L. *Paw Paw Lake, Michigan (Images of a Lake)*, Southwestern Michigan Publications, Coloma, Michigan: Southwestern Michigan Publications, 1996.

Rasmussen, Roderick L. *Paw Paw Lake, Michigan: A 100 Year Resort History (1890s–1990s)*, Coloma, Michigan: Southwestern Michigan Publications, 1994.

Ray, Lorraine. "Lew Sarett was Man of Many Facets." *News-Palladium*, May 8, 1964.

Reber, L. Benj. *History of St. Joseph*. St. Joseph, Michigan: St. Joseph Chamber of Commerce, 1925.

Region of Three Oaks. The Edward K. Warren Foundation. Three Oaks, Michigan, 1939.

Rockhold, Wanda. *Chips Fell in the Valley*. Benton Harbor Centennial Committee, 1966.

Roth, Walter. "Camp Avodah." *Chicago Jewish History*. Summer 1999.

St. Joseph and Benton Harbor, Twin Cities of The East Shore and their Multiples of Attractions. 1893.

Sanborn Map Company. "Sanborn Insurance Map." New York: Sanborn Map Company of New York, 1926.

Schafer, Kathleen. *Baroda: The Story of a Small Place*. Baroda Centennial Committee, 1992.

Schultz, Robert E. *Twin City Trolleys: A History of Street Railways and also Interurbans in Benton Harbor and St. Joseph, Michigan*. Las Vegas, Nevada, 1984.

Schultz, Alan. "Silver Beach, 1891 to 1975." *Michigan History*. June/August 1979.

"Silver Beach Boxing Contest." *The Evening Post*. June 2, 1905.

"Silver Beach Breaks Record." *The Evening Post*. 1906.

Sizer, Jack. *Birchwood Summers*. 1991.

Souvenir History of Coloma, Michigan.

Spink, John. "Spink's Spring Bluff Resort," unpublished one-page document, August 1991.

Standard Atlas of Berrien County, Michigan. Chicago: George Ogle & Co., 1903.

Stark, Mabel. *Trails from Shingle Diggin's*. R.W. Patterson Printing Co., 1977.

"State Troops May Come if Necessary to Establish Rigid Small Pox Quarantine." *News-Palladium*, August 10, 1909.

Taylor, R. James. *200 Years: Joanna Southcott—1792 through the City of David, 1992*. Benton Harbor: 1992.

Taylor, R. James. *Mary's City of David*. Benton Harbor: Mary's City of David, 1996.

Thomopoulos, Elaine. *St. Joseph and Benton Harbor*. Charleston, S.C.: Arcadia Publishing, 2003.

Thomopoulos, Elaine. Paper on "Summer Memories," presented at the Oral History Conference, Bethesda, Maryland, November, 2003.

Tolhuizen, James A. "History of the Port of St. Joseph-Benton Harbor." Thesis submitted to the Faculty of the School of Graduate Studies in partial fulfillment of the Degree of Master of Arts at Western Michigan University. Kalamazoo, Michigan, 1965.

VanderMolen, Francie. "From Tents to Midwest's Largest Fair." Unknown local newspaper, 1995.

Vegetarian Cook Book. Benton Harbor: City of David, undated.

Wallace, San Dee. "Walking Tour Demonstrates Historic Area," *Herald Palladium*, February 10, 1987.

Warner, Clarence. *Recollections of Benton Harbor*. Date unknown (before 1957).

"Warren Dunes Nature Trail." Michigan Department of Natural Resources. March, 2001.

"Warren Dunes State Park." Brochure produced by the Department of Natural Resources, Parks and Recreation, 2001.

"The Waters that Healed," *Herald Palladium*, March 8, 1992.

"Waves Batter Higman Park Inn." *Benton Harbor News-Palladium*, October 23, 1929.

The Way We Were In Union Pier, Michigan, Union Pier Reunion, September 21, 2002.

"The Way We Were In Union Pier, Michigan, Memories," *The Red Arrow Review*, August, September, October, November, 1993.

Winslow, D.A. *History of St. Joseph*. 1869.

Zerler, Glenn and Kathryn. *Blossomtime Festival, Southwest Michigan*. Benton Harbor: Blossomtime Inc., 1995.

Zerler, Kathryn. *On the Banks of the Ole St. Joe*. St. Joseph: St. Joseph Today, 1990.

Zerler, Kathryn. "A Sentimental Journey to Silver Beach," *St. Joseph: A Special Place on the Lake*, April 26, 1993.

Zerler, Kathryn. *Talk of the Towns*. St. Joseph, 1991.

Websites: "A Brief History of Camp S. Betz," calcouncil.org; "Harbor Country," harborcountry.org/harbert; "A Historical Remembrance by Ruth Magdzinski," pinegarth.com; "History of the Lakeside Inn," Lakesideinns.com; "Inn at Union Pier," innatunionpier.com; "Israelite House of David," israelitehouseofdavid.org/park.html; "Mary's City of David," maryscityofdavid.org; "Welcome to Union Piers Past." unionpierspast.com; "Saint Chrysostom's Episcopal Church," saintc.org; and "Michigan, the Great Lakes State," InfoMi.com; "Vacations and Resorts," college.hmco.com.

Personal and phone interviews with author: Margie Andrews, Ted Bachunas and Helen Bachunas, Gene Capozio, Jane Granzow Miles, Elizabeth and Herb Hahn, Dr. Nick Poulos, Marlene Owens Rankin, David Stacey, Rick Rasmussen, Gintaras Kaiteris, and Ruth Magdzinski.

Other interviews: Interviews conducted by the Berrien County Historical Association and Columbia College Chicago: Celia Alexopoulos (by Kevin Gruber, December 20, 2002), Mike Economos (by Kelsey Hoff, December 20, 2002), Al Coulolias (by Michael Obrerhoitzer, December 4, 2002), Aphrodite Demeur (by Ada Bjorklund Moore, December 7, 2002), Adrienne Georgandas (by Kelly McNulty, December 20, 2002), Janice Georgandas (by Marija Knezevic, December 20, 2002), Vaso Powers (by April Mauritzen, January 9, 2003), John Rassogianis (by Melissa Ann Peifer, January 10, 2003), Eugenia Seifer (by Shaneka Smith, December 20, 2002), Aphrodite Tatooles (by Despina Damianides, December 20, 2002), and James Tatooles (by Eva McCann, January 10, 2003).

Interviews conducted by the Fort Miami Historical Society: Jane Granzow Miles (by Jean Dalzell, June Runyan, and Lewis Filstrup, August 7, 1991); Emil Tosi (by Gwenn Schadler, James Skinner, and Lewis Filstrup, July 1994); Ted and Helen Bachunas (by Elaine Thomopoulos, August 12, 2004.)